SAILORS' JOURNEY INTO WAR

⚓

Robert A. Maher, circa 1941

Sailors' Journey into War

ROBERT A. MAHER

AND

CAPTAIN JAMES E. WISE, JR.

THE KENT STATE UNIVERSITY PRESS

Kent, Ohio, and London, England

Library of Congress Catalog Card Number 97-30538
ISBN 0-87338-583-7
Manufactured in the United States of America

04 03 02 01 00 99 98   5 4 3 2 1

Portions of this book appeared as a two-part article in the Summer and September/ October 1993 issues of *Naval History* magazine. Reprinted by permission of the U.S. Naval Institute.

Library of Congress Cataloging-in-Publication Data

Maher, Robert A., 1918–
    Sailors' journey into war / Robert A. Maher and James E. Wise, Jr.
        p.   cm.
    Portions of this book appeared as a two-part article in the summer
and Sept./Oct. 1993 issues of "Naval history" magazine.
    Includes bibliographical references and index.
    ISBN 0-87338-583-7 (cloth : alk. paper) ∞
    1. Maher, Robert A., 1918–   . 2. World War, 1939–1945—Naval
operations, American.   3. World War, 1939–1945—Personal narratives,
American.   4. Sailors—United States—Biography.   5. United States.
Navy—Biography.   I. Wise, James E., 1930–   . II. Title.
D773.M34   1998
940.54'5973'092—dc21   97-30538
    [B]   CIP

British Library Cataloging-in-Publication data are available.

Dedicated to our gallant comrades of the USS *Borie* who gave their lives for their country

⚓

Alford, Opal, S2c, USNR

Blouch, Warren, S2c, USNR

Bonfiglio, Charles, S2c, USNR

Blane, Max, S2c, USNR

Brown, Morrison, Lt., USNR

Cituk, Frank, PhM1c, USN

Concha, Domingo, SF2c, USNR

DeMaio, Harold, CWT, USNR

Duke, Frank, RT1c, USNR

Fields, James, F1c, USNR

Francis, Lawrence, S2c, USN

Kiszka, Joseph, WT2c, USNR

Lombardi, Joseph, F1c, USNR

Long, Ralph, CCS, USN

Lord, Robert, Lt. (jg), USNR

McKervey, Francis, Y2c, USNR

Medved, William, F1c, USNR

Mulligan, William, SC2c, USNR

Pouzar, Daniel, F2c, USNR

Pruneda, Aguinaldo, COX, USNR

Shakerly, William, CQM, USNR

St. John, Richard, Ens., USNR

Swan, Frank, F2c, USN

Tull, Richard, S2c, USN

Tyree, D. L., S2c, USNR

Wallace, Andrew, F1c, USNR

Winn, James, S1c, USNR

Contents

⚓

Foreword

⚓

I first corresponded with Bob Maher in 1986. I was doing research on German U-boat warfare in the Atlantic for an article I was writing and ran across the remarkable story of the old four-stacker, the USS *Borie* (DD215).

In October 1943 the *Borie* fought the *U405* in a fierce battle north of the Azores Islands. The nighttime action saw the two vessels locked together after the *Borie* rammed the U-boat. Crewmen from both warships fired at each other from point-blank range using any weapons available. The U-boat eventually went down. Though victorious, the *Borie* was so badly damaged during the melee that she had to be abandoned the following day and was sunk by our own ships.

Until the time the United States was able to form and deploy hunter-killer groups such as baby flattops with destroyer escorts, the Germans wreaked havoc in the Atlantic. More than nine hundred merchant vessels were lost to U-boat attacks in 1942, a particularly devastating year for the Allies in that theater. The following year, with the advent of improved antisubmarine technology and more air and seaborne hunters, the allies lost but three hundred ships (only sixty were lost during the last half of that year). The war against U-boats had turned in favor of the Allies and, for all practical purposes, that war was over except for a few final forays by Grand Admiral Karl Doenitz's dwindling U-boat forces.

I wanted to learn more about the *Borie* incident because it was unique. I searched the standard World War II naval histories and found brief descriptions of the battle but no firsthand accounts. Although I was determined to pursue the story and was able to contact the former skipper of the ship in Terre Haute, Indiana, I got distracted by other projects. It wasn't until I read of a 1986 *Borie* reunion in the U.S. Naval Institute *Proceedings* that I seriously began to track the story and its players once again.

I immediately contacted the coordinator of the event, who referred me to the group's historian, and he eventually suggested that I contact Bob Maher, who was aboard the *Borie* during the battle.

Bob is a charming man with a delightful, dry wit. He is also a fine writer. He had already written a memoir of his naval service and was kind enough to send me a copy. In it he wrote a minute-by-minute account of the battle. Bob saw it all because as the leading fire-control man and gun-director pointer he was stationed immediately above the bridge. He recalled that it was like watching a movie unfold before him.

After reading the memoir, I thought the battle action segment of the memoir would make a good article for the Naval Institute's magazine, *Naval History*. Working together, we submitted a manuscript to the magazine's editor; the article was published in 1993 as a two-issue piece. It was so well received that Bob and I were honored as Authors of the Year by *Naval History* magazine.

I was completing a book at the same time we were composing the article and had little time to think more about Bob's memoir. However, it was always in the back of my mind that his story was more than the battle incident; it was a tale of young men who were taken from the comfort of their families and hometowns and cast into a war of unimagined proportions. The *Borie* crew was no different from those aboard other American warships. The men bonded, learned their jobs well, and went into combat with determination and, often, great courage.

I reread Bob's story several times and proposed to him that we do a book together. I believed the memoir contained too much valuable history and human interest to be discarded and not be passed on to future generations of Americans who wanted to learn about the sea war from one who had been there.

The book includes much of the subtle wit that is purely Bob Maher. In addition to enjoying the intensity of the sea battle, readers will get numerous chuckles from his many anecdotes that were a part of the sailor's life as he and his shipmates endured periods of boredom and moments of frightening combat while far at sea with no end of the war in sight.

The book is rightly dedicated to twenty-seven *Borie* men who were lost after abandoning ship during heavy seas following the night action. None were lost during the battle. Bob himself, however, was nearly killed while being rescued.

Captain James E. Wise, Jr., USN (Ret.)

Acknowledgments

⚓

I wish to extend my deepest thanks and appreciation to my wife, Sandy. Her time, efforts, and especially her understanding made the completion of this book possible.

Robert A. Maher

PART ONE

⚓

Kearny, New Jersey

September 1939 – November 1940

Up to now, 1939 hadn't been much different from previous years, except for the additional freedom that my mother and father gradually granted as I grew older. Now twenty years old and still living with my parents, I had to live by their rules, which had relaxed to the point where I could pretty much come and go as I pleased as long as I didn't embarrass the family name. Since I am writing this in 1994, I can see some eyebrows being raised by young folks as they ask, "What does he mean? Did he have to ask his parents' permission to lead his own life?"

I can understand their confusion in a time when condoms are made available in our school systems so students can have "safe" sex. The only place for students to get them in the 1930s was from a little fat guy standing on the corner near the high school. If he was caught, he was arrested for contributing to the delinquency of a minor. Hell, he didn't do much business because most of the guys I knew bought them just for bragging rights. A fellow bought one, put it in his wallet, and there it stayed until he was married or he bought a new wallet, whichever came first. But not to worry, this is not going to be a story of "the way we did it in the good old days." Come to think of it, we probably did it the same way it's done today.

September 24, 1938, my twentieth birthday, to September 1, 1939, was a fun year for me. I was making a little more money ($80 a month), which left me some spending money after I paid room and board to my mother and train fare to New York City from Kearny, New Jersey. I was able to have a few drinks during the week and play bar shuffleboard, not to be confused with deck shuffleboard. Since we couldn't afford to drink beer all night, my best friend at that time, Shrimpy Graham, and I went to the movies almost every night before we gathered at the local tavern with the others for shuffleboard. In time Shrimpy and I became famous for our critiques of current movies. We even started a "stinker" list that eventually became just as sought after as the list of recommended pictures.

The best part of the year, in both 1939 and 1940, was summer, starting with Decoration Day (now called Memorial Day) and ending on Labor Day. A gang of us spent every weekend at the New Jersey shore in Belmar. We left right after work, rain or shine, on Friday and came home on Sunday night, late.

We had fun, but it was expensive. We all stayed in cabins (two dollars per night) because there were no motels at that time. Sometimes the cabins were in rows, with common walls in between that were so thin you could hear someone sneeze—and anything else that might be going on. Often the cabins were used only for an hour or two. I never could understand why only couples did the short rental bit. I guess they used the cabins just to change into their bathing suits, although I never saw anyone come out in a suit. Oh well, that is another of life's mysteries.

In good weather we spent the whole day on the beach, riding the waves on our stomachs, and I really mean riding. We would go out as far as we could, wait for a large wave about to break, then start to swim. When our bodies got caught in the crest of the wave, we pulled our arms back and in against our bodies. It was a wild ride, with only our heads and shoulders showing as the wave crashed toward the beach, the equivalent of today's body surfing. If we were lucky and locked on to a really good wave we got sand burns as our chins and chests rode right out of the wave onto the sand at the edge of the water.

If the weather was poor but not raining, we played stickball on the beach using a tennis ball and a broom handle for a bat. The two best players were always captains, and they took turns choosing players for their respective sides. It made no difference to me who chose first because I was always picked next to last unless some girls played with us. Everyone would rather have the girls on the opposite side, not because we cared who would win but because we liked to watch them run.

On Saturday evening we walked the boardwalk and ate our hearts out watching pretty girls dance, mostly with other girls. Only one of our group could dance, and boy, did he have it made. *Yes!* The rest of us drooled while we watched them jitterbug, their skirts swinging as their bobby socks and saddle shoes kept time with the music of the big bands. How often I kicked myself in those days for not taking dance lessons when I was twelve. My mother had offered to pay for them, even though money was very short, but dancing was only for sissies.

One other fun thing Shrimpy and I did was "cruise." Shrimpy bought a beautiful car, a 1929 Model A Ford coupe. It had two doors and only two seats. The window on the passenger's side was missing, but the handle for running it up and down was still in working order. Turning it produced a loud staccato noise that sounded like a gangster's machine gun. We would often whiz past a group of girls, the coupe emanating sounds like an attacking aircraft. For some reason, the girls were not impressed.

We used the car, except for football games, mostly to pick up girls. We lived in Kearny, but of course the prettiest girls lived across the river in Belleville so that's where we went hunting.

The time period between about 1938 and 1947 was called the Big Band Era. There were many large dance bands (twenty-five or more musicians) that played at large hotels for entertainment and dancing. Most of the bands were associated with a regular radio program, some entertaining on their own and some as support for well-known radio stars such as Jack Benny, George Burns, and others.

Each band had its own distinct style and its own loyal followers who could identify the band after only two or three notes. Of course, during these Depression years most people could enjoy the music of these bands only via radio. Only the rich could afford to attend the large affairs at beautiful hotels, but Shrimpy and I, living only a nickel trolley ride away from Newark, were able to enjoy all the big bands in person.

Not only was this period the Big Band Era, it was also the age of large, ornate, beautiful theaters that could hold thousands. Most of the bands had a "home port" in some large hotel or nightclub, such as the Copacabana in New York City, but they all played for the public, traveling around the country on an entertainment circuit and using those theaters. Newark had the Mosque, the most beautiful theater imaginable and, most important, reasonably priced. The cost was under one dollar, so Shrimpy and I could see all the bands up close. We never missed a show. After all these years I can still see and hear in my mind some of those bands as they performed. It was a wonderful and unforgettable experience for two poor young men.

While Shrimpy and I were enjoying ourselves in our own little world, things were happening outside our borders that should have awakened our nation but didn't. Everyone was preaching "America first." Let's solve our own problems and let the rest of the world go scratch.

In 1938 Adolf Hitler's Nazi Germany took Austria. It was a test of the rest of Europe to see what would happen. Nothing happened. Also in 1938, the Nazis intensified their violent anti-Jewish measures. When they received only token complaints from the world, the atrocities against the Jews became increasingly more horrible and finally ended with the murder of millions.

In late 1938 and early 1939, Germany split up Czechoslovakia and received only a few rumbles from the rest of Europe.

In 1939 Italy invaded Albania.

Of course, our "beach gang" didn't even talk about these events. I doubt if we ever got past the sports page in the newspaper, but after I read the history of those times, including old newspapers, it appeared the whole population cried out, "Stay home, these are not our problems!" Even my boyhood hero, Col. Charles Lindbergh (the first man to fly solo across the Atlantic Ocean), advocated isolationism. "Lindy" was the first man to be presented with *Time* magazine's Man of the Year award in 1927, so you can see that the nation held him and his opinions in high esteem.

Lindbergh visited Hitler's Germany, and on his return, he told the nation that Hitler was building up his military forces only for self-defense; America had nothing to fear from Germany. He also said that Germany's air force was so powerful that Europe could not contain Germany if a war came to pass. His stature as a national hero gave his opinion credibility. He was to be proven wrong, but only because the United States was ultimately drawn into the war. Unfortunately, his statements and other matters delayed the buildup of our defense system at a most critical time in the history of the United States. It wasn't until after the war that people discovered that Lucky Lindy had accepted Hitler's invitation on the advice of our State Department. He was sent to assess the strength of the Luft-waffe. When he returned, he simply told the truth as he saw it, even though Americans, including me, didn't like what they heard. We learned after the war ended that Lindbergh offered his services immediately after the attack on Pearl Harbor. He served as a combat test pilot in the Pacific, completing fifty missions and shooting down one Japanese airplane. So it seems that the nation owed him an apology.

We all put our heads in the sand and hoped the problems around the world would go away. They didn't.

Soon after graduation from Kearny High School in 1937, I began work-ing for the Mutual Life Insurance Company in downtown New York. I hated the job, but we were in the middle of the Depression and it was the only one I could get. Forget that I had graduated in the top ten of my high school class after mastering the most difficult course in the school, the scientific, academic college program. Scholarships were hard to come by and there were no advisers to help us obtain those that were available. Luckily my father had a friend who was an officer in the insurance com-pany, and he helped me get a job. Although it wasn't what I had planned for my future, it was a job.

I started at the magnificent salary of fifty-five dollars a month, but that included a free full lunch, every day, in the company dining room. Every-one had his own time, seat, and table for lunch. For a poor kid that was pretty good. Lunch was served by waitresses at a table with tablecloths, napkins, and a full set of dinnerware. Lunch was a pretty big deal for me because the only time I had been to a restaurant before then was to a small, local Chinese restaurant with my mother when I was twelve years old.

By the summer of 1939 I had accepted my position for what it was, and I was doing a good job. I enjoyed working in the city, which was nothing like it became in the early 1960s. There were all kinds of shops and restaurants, including the famous Horn and Hardart's cafeteria where everything cost a nickel. People put a coin into a slot and then removed the food from behind a glass door. What my fellow workers and I liked best were the nearby bars where, with a few beers, we could have complimentary corned beef and cabbage, roast beef sandwiches, pretzels, pickles, and lots of other food, depending on the season. That gave us variety in our choice of eating companions without putting a dent in our nonexistent budgets. After we ate, there were many places to walk during the remainder of our lunch hour: East River had its outside clam bars and a place to sit and watch the girls go by. The aquarium was, I believe, the largest or second largest in the world at the time. The financial district (Wall Street) was always an exciting place to observe. If the boss wasn't at work, there was even time to take a ferryboat ride out to the Statue of Liberty.

Occasionally, but not often because of money and train schedules, I would go out for the evening with friends in the office. One of our favorite spots was the Radio City Music Hall in New York City, which opened December 27, 1932. The country was in the depths of the Great Depression, so it was an optimistic and courageous enterprise. On the great stage, entertaining an audience of six thousand, were the dance immortals Ray Bolger (the scarecrow in *The Wizard of Oz*) and Martha Graham, the Flying Wallendas (high-wire and trapeze performers), and a troupe of beautiful young women dancing and high-kicking with a rhythmic precision that would make them world famous. Of course, everyone knows them as the Rockettes, and they still star in Radio City's Christmas Spectacular today.

My desk was in a large office area that had workspace for about one hundred people. The working rules were very loose so we could walk around and talk to each other as long as our work was done by the end of the day. One might excuse our beach gang's disinterest in world affairs because of our youth, but looking back, I realize that my co-workers, who ranged in age from eighteen to sixty-four, with most over thirty, showed no more interest than we did.

The "beach gang" in Belmar, 1939.

As the summer of 1939 came to an end, life went on as usual. The 1939–40 New York World's Fair was in full swing. During the week I was only five minutes away by subway (a five-cent fare) so I knew I could go whenever it was the right time for me. I never did make it. A picture of some of our "beach gang" on the beach in Belmar in 1939 shows me standing on the left. Next to me, with the sun helmet, is a cousin of Johnny Parks. Next to him is Buddy, who was not one of my favorite people. Next to him is my pal Shrimpy, and you can see why he was called that. I should point out that it wasn't very smart for anyone to make snide remarks about his size because he would get a face full of knuckles, no matter how big he was. Next to Shrimpy is Joe Giunta. I would go out with Joe if for some reason Shrimpy couldn't make it to the beach. Joe also had a car, and what a car for a bunch of young bucks. It was a gangster's car, a white Hudson four-door convertible, and the top was down most of the time. It was very, very long, and its hood extended forever. There was about two feet of space between the radiator and the engine. It was the perfect car for picking up girls; however, that worked only if Joe was alone—at least that's what he said. I know when I was with Joe, the Hudson didn't work any better than Shrimpy's 1929 Ford.

In the front row, the guy on the left is a fellow we saw only on the beach. He wasn't from the Kearny area; he had just started to hang out with us. It was a good thing, too. He was a little older and had a good job and a beautiful car. He also had the handicap of being handsome, big, with a great body and ugly, natural curly hair. If we did see him at night, he was always with a pretty girl and dancing in the pavilion. I'm sure he made out because he had a nicer car than the other guys. In spite of his obvious physical faults, he was a nice guy, and we liked him. Next to him is Andy, the guy with the teeth. He wasn't one of my favorites either, but I liked to have him around because I could play ball better than he could. Of course, everyone knew you couldn't succeed in picking up girls with three guys in a car, so he was never asked. He brought his own car, but I soon realized he wasn't doing as well as the rest of us. How did I draw that conclusion? The clue came one Saturday when he told us he would be leaving the beach early to drive to Scranton, Pennsylvania, to go to a whorehouse. That's what they called them. "Call girls" and "ladies of the evening" were unknown terms until the affluent 1960s. The drive to Scranton was a long one, maybe four hours, in those days. There were no superhighways or parkways, only two-lane roads with stop lights and city traffic. I guess he thought it was worth it because after that he periodically took off early from the beach on Saturday afternoons. He was the only guy I knew in the group who definitely was having sex. I suspect the hunk was, but I'm not sure.

Front right in the photo is Johnny Parks. He was another of my favorite companions, and we occasionally went out together. He and his cousin were natives of Scotland, and they both had nice Scottish brogues. Three of these nice young men would be dead within five years.

Look at the picture closely. See my belly button? I think this was about the second year that men wore that type of bathing suit. Note that Shrimpy's suit is connected to his trunks, and mine was supposed to be. A zipper connected to the trunks for ease of dressing, but if you got caught with your top off you would be kicked off the beach. The second time you would lose your beach admittance badge. The life guards took turns walking the beach, looking for guys who dressed shamelessly like that. (Those same life guards would probably suffer cardiac arrest observing today's beach attire.)

As mentioned earlier, Hitler's Germany had been taking little bites of Europe, testing the rest of the world. No country, especially the United States, had objected violently, so Hitler decided to take a big bite.

In the early morning hours of September 1, 1939, German troops began to move swiftly across the Polish border. What followed was the first full-scale demonstration of blitzkrieg (lightning war). The invasion had been preceded by Luftwaffe Stuka dive-bombers attacking airfields, bridges, and lines of communications. The most horrible thing to see (in newsreels in the theaters) were those airplanes, in almost vertical dives, dropping bombs on brave but pathetic Polish soldiers on horseback who were charging Panzer tanks. The world was on an inevitable course to World War II.

What impact did those events have on me and my friends? Not much.

Labor Day always ended our group beach forays, so we soon were back into our mostly inexpensive activities. Shrimpy and I started reviewing movies, playing shuffleboard, and touring for girls in Belleville.

Life, for the rest of 1939 and the winter of 1940, went on pretty much as it had: we drank beer, cruised for noncooperating girls, and went to movies. I also had one new experience. My co-workers introduced me to the world of burlesque in late spring or early summer of 1940, a harmless vice that could have been habit-forming except for the cost and the late hour I arrived home.

Although there were some sleazy burlesque troupes, the shows in New York's Times Square district were, for the most part, top-quality productions. Most of the prominent comedians of the 1940s and 1950s got their start in burlesque: Milton Berle, Henny Youngman, George Burns, and others.

The show was made up of comedy skits and elaborate dance numbers with well-known strippers backed up by a dance group in skimpy (very) but gorgeous costumes. All the girls were beautiful and bare breasted, not that this had anything to do with why we went to the burlesque theater. We went only for the comedy acts and the jokes. Sure we did.

It's funny how, after fifty years, I still remember some of the stars of those shows and their attributes: Carrie Finnel for the way she could make two tassels swing and rotate, even in opposite directions, just by wiggling her shoulders; Rose La Rose, who didn't have to do anything but stand there; Lily St. Cyr, who used a python snake as part of her stripping act; Margie Hart, who was billed as the fastest stripper (and boy, was she ever!); and of course the person who turned striptease dancing into an art form, Sally Rand. She became world famous doing her fan dance, sans clothes, at the Chicago World's Fair. She was so good, rumor had it that Ginger Rogers, Cyd Charisse, and all those other Hollywood dancers applied for job insurance.

Even while my friends and I were enjoying these art forms (cruising for girls, strippers, beer drinking, bar shuffleboard, watching girls play ball), fate was churning things about so that, in the not-too-distant future, all of us would be going our separate ways, never to see each other again. In fact, about that time something happened that would soon affect me directly. On June 19, 1940, President Franklin D. Roosevelt signed the Two-Ocean Navy Bill. That act authorized the greatest expansion in our naval history: 1,325,000 tons.

Thursday, August 1, 1940, was a hot evening, and I was sitting on the front porch talking with my mother. A car, driven by Whitey Meikle, stopped in front of us. That was the beginning of one of the most important periods of my life, although I didn't know it then.

Shrimpy Graham, Phil Graham, Bob Black, and Herb Granquist also were in the car. Herb leaned out and called, "Hey Bob, come on. We're all going over to Jersey City to join the Naval Reserves." Hell, I didn't even know what the Naval Reserves were, but I thought if all these guys wanted to join, it must be a good idea. When I asked Mother what she thought of the idea, she told me to make up my own mind; I was a big boy now. I did.

I hopped into the car and off we went to Jersey City, with the fellows telling me why this was a good idea. Although none of us (as I recall) expected to go off to war, we did know that it was highly likely we would have to go into military service soon because a draft bill had been proposed to Congress and its passage was certain. It was called the Burke-Wadsworth Act, creating selective service for all men over the age of eighteen. THAT WAS US! Draft registration was to begin next month, and by joining the reserves we would be assured of naval service, which I agreed sounded better than infantry.

When we got to the Reserve Armory, it was crowded. The Armory was a big old ship, and I do mean big and OLD. It was called the USS *Newton* and had been converted for that duty. Although it was afloat, it was never going to be a seagoing ship again. There was also an old (everything was old in those days) Coast Guard patrol boat, called the USS *Eagle 55,* and it was seagoing and was used for training. After Pearl Harbor *Eagle 55* was called back to active duty.

It seemed that every young man and his cousin had had the same good idea. We were separated into small groups for a rather laughable intelligence test; it was about as hard as this maze:

IN ⟶ ⟶ ⟶ OUT

We all got through the prerequisites and were herded into groups for our physicals, but not together. Although I had been the school's worst athlete, I had tried every sport and was used to large groups of naked men. I wasn't ready for that physical, however.

Picture this if you care to: two rows of naked men facing each other, a corpsman moving rapidly down the middle, looking side to side while performing "short arm" inspection which you watched until it was your turn; following him came two doctors, one for each line, probing the rear. I wonder if you can imagine what it feels like to stare into another's face while both of you are having your prostates massaged. You don't feel like asking, "So, how's your mother?" As soon as all the behinds were back to normal, the doctors went into reverse and came back down the lines checking for hernias. A nice touch was when the doctors split up and went down the same line, one in front and the other in back for the fastest stethoscope check I have ever had.

I was soon judged healthy enough to be a sailor and was sent on to a recruiting chief petty officer who, at first, treated me like a son. He asked me what I would like to be on board ship, and when I informed him that I would like to be a signalman he told me it would be no problem. He swore me in and when I had signed, he shouted, "GET OVER THERE!" I never did become a signalman. When we were accepted, we were given the opportunity to agree to one year of naval service if needed, and in return we would not have to register for the draft. I volunteered for one year of active duty.

Later, our gang got together to compare notes. Bob Black failed because of a funny scar caused by an operation. Phil Graham wasn't accepted because he wasn't a citizen. Whitey Meikle didn't make it because he was color blind, and Shrimpy Graham was too small. I don't remember why Herbie didn't make it. Guess who was the only one accepted? ME.

What happened to those guys? Herb became a fighter pilot in the South Pacific, Shrimpy became an army mule skinner in the Italian Alps, Bob Black finally got into the navy, Phil Graham held the first number called in the draft (158, picked by the secretary of war on October 29, 1940) and was in the army before I was called. Al Meikle became an army corpsman and made landings at North Africa, Sicily, Anzio, and Normandy.

But nothing was to happen for quite a while. We, as most other Americans did, went right on being fat, dumb, and happy—enjoying ourselves and the upward surge in the economy caused by the war in Europe. The war in Europe (called the phony war) was now almost a year old, but nothing much was going on. Looking back, I don't know how we could have been so naive as to think we wouldn't be caught up in it. Until the war broke out in Europe, we were a weak nation, and getting weaker, while the Axis powers were getting stronger. There was Japanese aggression in China and Italian aggression in Ethiopia, while the Germans had already shown their intentions. In addition, the Germans had trained their pilots both in Ethiopia and in the Spanish Civil War. It wasn't until late 1939 and early 1940 that President Roosevelt began to set in motion plans to help the Allies and improve our readiness. But most of us went on thinking that this was not our war, and many even went so far as to oppose preparing any defense system. Fortunately, the president was strong enough that we weren't completely helpless after Pearl Harbor. In September 1940, Roosevelt, alert to the worldwide threat imposed by Nazism, agreed to a momentous immediate exchange. In return for fifty old destroyers, Britain leased naval and air bases to the United States in its Western Hemisphere possessions: Newfoundland, Bermuda, the Bahamas, Jamaica, Antigua, St. Lucia, Trinidad, and British Guiana. Little did I know that in a few months I would be living aboard an old four-stack destroyer and would visit most of those bases. The army began conscription on September 16, 1940, for a one-year training period. Ho, ho. The navy and the marines stayed with voluntary enlistments. In December 1940, the Office of Production Management was established to extend all aid short of war to Great Britain and all antibelligerents. But hell, it wasn't our war, at least to most of us.

On November 19, 1940, when I returned to the office from lunch, I was told that Mr. Harding, my big boss, wanted to see me right away. I wondered what I had done now because he was a hard guy to work for. He told me that my mother had called and that I should go home at once because I had received a telegram telling me to report for active duty with the navy on November 21, Thanksgiving Day. So I left the service of the Mutual Life Insurance Company a short while later, holding a pen and pencil set that someone had scurried to find, ready to serve my country. I would never regret it.

Thanksgiving morning my brother, Ed, drove me to the *Newton* in the Nash heap, now his. When we got there everyone was milling around, waiting for instructions. About four hundred men had been called to active duty, and most of them had relatives or loved ones to see them off, so it was an emotional scene. I was happy and looking forward to some new and exciting adventures away from the dull insurance job.

While I waited, a huge man in uniform came up and said hello to Ed. Ed had worked on him many times as a football trainer. His name was Dick Wenz, and he was going to be on the same ship as I. He promised Ed he would watch out for me, and did that ever turn out to be a laugh, several times.

Dick meant well, but when we went aboard ship we soon discovered that everyone had their own jobs and problems that only they could handle. For reasons I don't understand, they issued us "rain or shine" box lunches (whatever that meant) and told us we could go home for the rest of the day. We were to report at the train station in Exchange Place, Jersey City, on Friday morning.

The train came, and amid mass confusion and more tears, we boarded. We left Exchange Place at 9:55 A.M. I don't remember much about the train ride, except eating the lunch, making friends, guessing how big the USS *Borie* was, and being excited about going to a foreign country, Panama. I also found out that most of the men in uniform didn't know any more than I did about naval customs. It seems that the Naval Reserve had expanded so quickly that most of these men had been in long enough to get uniforms but not to receive any real training. That fact was to be important to me very soon.

Dick Wenz, who had muscles on his muscles. He was to become our chief gunner's mate.

Ordered to leave Jersey City on November 22, 1940, was the 24th Division, Seventh Battalion, USNR. The men in uniform were organized reservists and as such were ordered to active duty. That mess of nonuniformed bodies at the end of the column were men who hadn't been in long enough to receive uniforms. See that fellow in the rear left with his hand on his hip? That's me. Even though I hated crowded lines and was not about to join that mess, I soon learned that when an officer orders you to do something, you do it.

PART TWO

⚓

I Report Aboard the USS *Borie (DD215)*
Panama Patrol

November 1940 – January 1943

We arrived at Cape Charles, Virginia, at 4:30 P.M. We prepared to board a boat for my first sea duty as a member of the U.S. Navy. In the ferry boat *Virginia Lee,* we sailed across the mighty Chesapeake Bay, arriving at Norfolk, Virginia, about 7:30 P.M. We were herded into buses and headed for Norfolk Naval Base, at the time the largest naval station in the world. By 8:30 P.M. we were in our temporary barracks where we found bunks, which we badly needed by then. That was another first for me—double-deck bunks. I wasn't used to sleeping looking at another guy's fanny. In only a couple of days, however, I was to find out that seeing only one guy's fanny was luxury. I went off to sleep thinking, boy, so far this hasn't been anything at all like the movies. I'm not sure (nor is anyone else I asked) if we were issued our gear that night or the next morning, but my recollection is that it was the next morning.

Upon awakening, I found we were in brand new buildings with new bunks and mattresses. But hell, it wasn't our war. It was time to make my first morning "head call" so I went in search of the toilet, which wasn't hard to find. What was hard to find though was a toilet with a door. I walked up and down the rows. No doors on the stalls! It must be because it was a new building. I went to three buildings before I finally realized that that's the way it was. I decided I would write to someone as soon as I was onboard the *Borie* and suggest they put doors on the toilets. When I did get aboard the *Borie,* I discovered there weren't any doors for toilets there, either. Hell, the *Borie* didn't even have toilets!

It didn't take a brick wall to fall on me. That's the way it was, and that's the way it was going to be for a long time. I put up with it, but I never got used to it. After breakfast we were issued our uniforms, bedding, and seabags. Since the navy began, if a sailor was transferred he had to carry all his gear with him. Besides his clothes, that included a mattress (heavy), blankets, sheets, and a hammock. At that time I weighed only about 130 pounds, and it was all I could do to lift the gear, never mind carry it to the ship. But I did. It wasn't until after Pearl Harbor that someone realized it would be a lot easier and cheaper to make the bedding a permanent part of the ship or station. Sailors had been saying that since the first one had to carry all of his gear—but what did they know?

We stayed at the barracks until Monday afternoon, November 25. About 2:30 P.M. we received orders to pack our gear and be ready to shove off. Wow! I'm in the navy only five days and look how "salty" I am—"gear" for clothes and "shove off" for go. But I was still saying pail instead of bucket and mop instead of swab. We shoved off and marched (sauntered and dragged is a better description) to a dock where a barge waited for us. It was a huge, flat, open barge with high sides that made it impossible to see where we were headed. We were packed so tightly that we were shoulder to shoulder and couldn't have fallen over if we smacked into a brick wall. A tugboat towed us through the cold and damp Hampton Roads to the Naval Station at Portsmouth, Virginia. I must say that so far my active duty in the navy had been somewhat less than glamorous, and I found myself thinking more and more of the comedians in the burlesque shows.

After about four hours, we disembarked at the shore end of a long dock with ships of all sizes tied up on both sides. First we had to sort out and distribute our gear, and then we were led out on the dock, as a group. We were all trying to pick out the *Borie,* which we hoped was the first ship we came upon, a beautiful cruiser. Wrong. When we finally came to the *Borie,* we found a tiny (compared to a cruiser) destroyer, and since it was, by now, about 2:00 A.M., only two men were visible on deck. On the dock we were split into two groups: deckhands (those who worked on deck) and "black gang" (those who worked below deck). I went aboard with the deckhands, not at all resembling a Hollywood sailor. I had envisioned myself looking like a recruiting poster, but with my hat over my ears and my baggy pants, I didn't quite make it.

The deckhand sleeping compartment was forward, under the bow and bridge, so we filed forward and then down two vertical ladders into our future home. It wasn't very impressive to those of us who had never seen the inside of a ship before. To say the ship was filthy was to be very kind. The compartment was about twenty-five feet long and thirty feet wide at the widest part and tapered down toward the bow. In this compartment were thirty-six bunks, thirty-six lockers that also served as seats, and two long mess tables that were used, in addition to eating, for writing, playing cards, and other activities. The bunks were folded up against the bulkhead during the day and dropped down at night. They were in stacks of three, and the preferred one was the top because the space between the others was so tight that to turn over a man had to push up on the other guy's behind; it took a while to get used to that. As I said, the double-decker bunks in the barracks were a luxury.

Forward crew's deck compartment. We had a lovely, spacious all-purpose living area. We could eat, sleep, play, and do all our personal things without the inconvenience of leaving. Here we are dining with close friends. On the right, the first clear face is Ed Malaney and next to him, eating, is me. My sleeping quarters are just over my head. I'm sitting on all my belongings, and at this time they're being guarded by my personal roaches. Our serving dishes were beautiful tureens—two of them can be seen in the foreground.

We hadn't had anything to eat since lunch so they (at that time I had no idea who "they" were) rousted the ship's cook out of his bunk and told him to feed us, which didn't please him at all! BAM! BAM! BAM! Loaves of bread started coming down the hatch from two decks above, with instructions to pass them around. I got one loaf, broke it open, and watched the biggest cockroach I had ever seen scurry across the mess table. Holding on to some bread, I waited for my first shipboard meal. Two young sailors, also ticked off for having been rousted, came down the ladders, both carrying a large pot, which they slammed down on the mess tables. My first meal at 2:00 A.M.? It was chili, which I couldn't eat because some of the things in it looked an awful lot like that roach I had let loose.

Now aboard ship, we were all assigned bunks and lockers, complete with cockroaches. Since most of us were really still civilians, it was an almost impossible task to get us organized into a manageable unit, but they did. We were divided into three watch divisions and then assigned work duties from 8:00 A.M. to 4:00 P.M., if we weren't on watch.

The navy had an apprentice system for earning ratings that worked quite well. For example, if a sailor wanted to become a gunner's mate (GM), he first had to get assigned to the gunnery division as an apprentice. Of course, nothing is called what it is in the navy; a sailor learning to be a gunner's mate was called a gunner's mate striker. He must now work with the already rated gunners, getting on-the-job training, and also study and pass written exams for advancement in rating. All the examinations were competitive, which eliminated, for the most part, the politics and favoritism found in the army, where the rates were by appointment. When you enlisted, you became an apprentice seaman, and as you learned basic seamanship you advanced to second class seaman (S2c) and then to first class seaman (S1c). At that time you had the opportunity to become a striker for a particular job, if one was open. Advancement was now in the petty officer ratings: PO3c, PO2c, PO1c, and Chief PO (CPO).

The men who washed dishes and served food aboard ship were called mess cooks (KP in the army), and on the first day I was told that I was going to be a mess cook striker, which didn't please me at all. I didn't see much of a future in becoming a mess cook petty officer, but I also couldn't see how I was going to avoid doing it. The first meal was hell! I served about thirty guys, running up and down two ladders from the galley to the men, carrying large pots that were called tureens. Neither I nor the eating men knew what was proper or what was expected from each other, so when some loudmouth at the far end of the table shouted at me to get him the blankety-blank sugar, I threw the whole tureen down the table; sugar trailed the whole length, covering both men and food. Funny thing was, it calmed everyone down, and the rest of the meal went fine. In spite of that, my thoughts were about my dismal future ahead as a permanent waiter.

I remember only a few things about the time we were tied up at the dock in Norfolk (called "Shit City" by all sailors). I was carrying a dishpan of dirty water to the fantail (stern) to throw it over the side when a voice from over the side called, "Hey Maaahhhhr, give us a hand." Putting my head over the side, I saw Eddie Johnson and Jimmy Allegri looking up at me from a stage (scaffold) supported by a block and tackle at each end. Wearing their new uniforms, pea jackets, and white hats, they were dumb enough to ask me to lower them down a little at a time, first one end and then the other. I informed them that I had been an insurance clerk and

Bill Schmalberger, mess cook. Of course the *Borie* had an automatic
dishwasher; at that time it was Bill. He made CPO in record time.

After dinner, quality recreation. Above, left to right, are Fred Cramer, Domingo Concha, and Bill Schmalberger. "Mingo" is sitting on my home, with my bunk at his back. ("I want to turn in now." "Forget it!") Mingo, loved by all, was to be lost in action.

didn't know a pulley from a soup spoon. You see, I was learning my present job. Anyway, they assured me that I could do it, and I did. Zip— followed by yells, and splashes. It was a long time before those guys became my best friends.

During the first couple of weeks aboard ship I found out that learning to be a sailor was easy. It must have been because almost at once the officers started to refer to me in ecclesiastical terms. On one of my early messenger watches, the PO of the watch told me to give a message to Captain Miller. Now, I knew he was our CO, but I also knew that he wasn't a captain, only a lieutenant commander. I wasn't going to fall for that joke, so when I addressed him I said, "Mr. Miller." He turned around, looked at me, and quietly said, "Jesus Christ, Mr. Miller." Wasn't that nice?

Not long after, while I was on watch again, the PO asked me if I knew how to ring the ship's bell. What's so big about ringing a bell? I told him sure, so he told me to go ring eight bells. I went to the bridge, grabbed the end of the clapper line, and started to ring. Bong, bong, bong, bong, until eight bongs had rung. Captain Miller stuck his head out of the chart room and gave me another "Jesus Christ." The funny thing is that I

Ed Johnson and Jim Allegri, who eventually came to like me, even when sober.

USS *Borie (DD215)*, original configuration. In December 1940 we headed for sea and a year's active duty in Panama. For many of us, that was our first time at sea.

received all those compliments, and I didn't even go to church. I was to get a lot more of them throughout the year.

While in Norfolk, I personally encountered prejudice for the first time. A favorite sign (honest) was DOGS AND SAILORS KEEP OFF THE GRASS, and we soon found that we weren't welcome in places like churches or nice restaurants—only in bars.

But this was nothing compared to the treatment blacks received. For me, it was a shock. You see, Kearny, New Jersey, was a completely white town. Up to the time I left, and long after, not one black family lived there so unless your parents taught you to be biased (my parents didn't), there was no reason to be prejudiced. For the first time in my life, I saw signs such as "White only" and "Negroes not allowed" while I was aboard the ferryboat *Virginia Lee*. Having separate facilities was only a small part of the treatment because the facilities themselves were quite different. For example, there were two water fountains aboard the ferry: the one for whites was beautiful, and the one for blacks was a piece of crap. None of us were sad when we finally left Norfolk and headed for sea and Panama.

You have to realize that most of us were street kids from middle-class to poor families. We hadn't been anywhere, and it wasn't likely that we were going to go any farther than the Jersey shore for a vacation, so heading for a distant shore was one of the biggest events of our lives so far. That first week was a wonderful, exciting, and difficult time. At first, the sea was calm, fortunately, and we started to learn to be sailors and to accept military discipline, but it wasn't easy. I remember only a few things about the trip to Panama. About a day or two out of Norfolk we entered the Gulf Stream, in daylight, and I couldn't believe the sudden change in temperature from winter to summer and the demarcation line where the ocean changed from nondescript green to beautiful royal blue. Now men began to see flying fish; that is, everyone but me. The crew pointed them out to me, but I never could see them. I started to think those guys were putting me on until, finally, one landed on the bow deck and someone brought it to me. Hell, I never would have seen one of those things! Every time a cry of "There goes one" was heard, I would look around for a sail-fish, tarpon, or swordfish. Flying fish were only about ten inches long, had flimsy small wings, and flew short distances about a foot above the water. How the heck should I know?

Near Cuba we entered the Windward Passage, a strait between eastern Cuba and northwestern Haiti, where we found that the ocean was always rough. In the morning I scraped and wire-brushed rust off the deck of the galley deck house as the ship began to roll and pitch with the changing sea. The area I was cleaning was directly above a vent from the galley below and I spent the better part of an hour breathing pork chop fumes. I swear that the cook purposely cooked greasy pork chops for our first meal at sea. This was just before going on lookout watch in the crow's nest for the first time. The crow's nest was a barrel-like unit, entered from the bottom; it was reached by climbing a skinny ladder up a fifty-foot mast, and it rolled about twenty degrees to either side. Nothing to it for a white collar insurance clerk. Before going aloft, I was told that if I got seasick I shouldn't use the voice tube because that would upset the captain—and I didn't want to do that again. I had already upset him when I bonged out eight bells. Of course he wasn't too thrilled when I hung the Union Jack upside down while in Norfolk, either.

I wasn't up there long when my stomach began to churn. I looked down on the bridge and saw Captain Miller's shiny head as he walked back and forth. NO! I looked at my brand new white hat. But the decision was soon made for me—sweeping out in a graceful arc from mast to stern, I splattered a group of sunbathers on the afterdeckhouse, who then made a mad dash, all trying at once to get down the one ladder. A new friend,

Stan Hull, was on watch also, on that same afterdeckhouse, and he couldn't leave. He had what was called the emergency wheel watch, a man ready to take over in case the main steering gear broke down while maneuvering. A piece of glop landed in his hat, and that was to do him in later. After heaving, I felt okay again, so when I saw heads appear from around the corner, I gave the hands clasped above the head sign indicating that it was safe to go back up again. Wrong! One more sweep cleared the deck house for the rest of the afternoon, except for Stan Hull.

The second two hours of the four-hour watch was rotated, so I came down from the crow's nest and Stan started up the narrow ladder getting the smell from his hat all the while. He made it halfway up and stopped. Soon the boatswain of the watch (the man in charge of lookouts) asked him what the hell he was doing. Stan croaked, "I'm too sick to go up and too sick to come down." The boatswain and another man had to climb up, pry him loose, and bring him down. Neither Stan nor I were of any use for the rest of the trip to Panama. In fact, I became so bad that I climbed out on a flagstaff from the stern and hung there with waves from the wake washing over me while men yelled for me to come in before I was washed overboard. I replied that I didn't care, and I really didn't. I got seasick many times, but I learned how to avoid it most of the time so it wasn't a big problem from then on. Some fellows (not many) never did get over it and had to be transferred to shore duty.

There was only one time that all but two of the crew had some degree of seasickness, and that was a horrifying experience. We got caught in a hurricane in the Atlantic (the same one that tore down the Steel Pier in Atlantic City), and with waves about thirty feet high we rolled over a measured fifty-seven degrees, all the while pitching fore and aft because we had great difficulty keeping the ship heading into the waves and wind. I know, because I was the helmsman. Green water rushing over the bow tore one of our lifeboats away, bent one-inch pipe stanchions, and broke all the windows on the bridge. I had to be tied to the helm so I wouldn't be swept away from the wheel, and many times my feet left the deck. Everyone was sick, but we all had to do our jobs if we were to survive.

We arrived at the navy base in Coco Solo, the Atlantic side of the U.S. Canal Zone, on a beautiful sunny day, and as the lines were secured to the dock, my sickness disappeared. That was to be our home port for almost two years, though we had volunteered for only one.

It was mid-December, and for almost all of us it was our first experience of being in a warm climate in the wintertime. We loved it. The first

Comrades in seasickness: Stan and me on Far Fan Beach, Panama. We became, and still are, good friends.

week we spent as much time as possible swimming, but when we found that every day was the same—sunny, hot, and humid with rain in the afternoon—it lost its appeal. We even got used to being caught in heavy showers and didn't even try to get under cover because we knew we would be dry within minutes after the rain stopped.

My high school Spanish became a worthwhile investment because few of the Panamanians spoke English. One evening while I was having dinner in a nice restaurant in Santiago, Cuba, Fred Cooper came to my table with a gorgeous, black-haired woman of Spanish extraction. She had flashing black eyes and smooth, perfectly white skin. I couldn't believe my eyes, although Fred was a good-looking guy. He informed me that she couldn't speak a word of English and asked if I would try to talk her into going out with him. After I talked with her for a little while, she agreed, but only if I would go along with them and her girlfriend. I decided to take a chance and discovered that her girlfriend was even more beautiful.

We left the restaurant, and when we got outside I found that a cab had already been hired. Another shipmate, Joe San Phillip, was there with another girl. The driver took us out of the city to a good-sized house, and

Our first liberty in a foreign country, and we're making football poses in a park! At front center is Eddie Johnson; at left is me; the rear three are (left to right) Jim Allegri, Bill Geary, and Bill Shakerly. Shakerly was to be lost in action, and Geary was to leave the *Borie* for sub duty. He was aboard the sub that fired the first shot (a torpedo) in the Battle of Leyte Gulf.

did we ever have a party. We were there overnight, and when, shortly after daybreak, it was time to go, we discovered the driver had slept in the car. He drove to the girls' homes first. It was funny. All three lived on the same street in a nice suburb, and as we approached their houses they ducked their heads so they wouldn't be seen and carried their shoes so they wouldn't be heard entering their homes. Back at the ship the driver charged us each only ten dollars for the evening. That date alone was worth the four years I spent studying Spanish.

A few days after we arrived in Panama, Lt. (jg) Paul Woerner, the gunnery officer, called me to his cabin. He asked if I would like to be a fire-control striker, and as much as I disliked being a waiter, I told him that I wouldn't really like to be down below taking care of the boilers in the fire rooms. I hadn't been in those rooms yet, and I didn't care to if I didn't have to. He laughed and told me that a fire-control man was responsible for the maintenance and upkeep of all the equipment used to aim and fire the guns and torpedoes, and he had called on me because I was one of only a few men who had the necessary math background for the job. I did have an A average for four years of math that included trigonometry, which is the basis for solving fire-control problems. Good-bye mess cooking and hello range finders, electronics, telescopes, gyros, and a whole new world, very different from my insurance world and much more fun. That chance appointment was to set me up for an exciting career when I left the navy five years later.

I had met Lieutenant Woerner some weeks earlier when, after being accepted into the battalion, I was told to report to him in his office and inform him that I had been assigned to his division. I knocked on his door, and when it opened I found myself staring into his navel. He was a huge, former Naval Academy football player. Looking down on me, he said, "My God, why do I get all the little guys?" Before he left the ship to end the war as a football coach at the Naval Academy, he offered me an appointment to the Academy. He was flabbergasted when I told him that I was twenty-two years old and therefore ineligible.

Enter Smitty. The head of the fire-control gang was a nineteen-year veteran by the name of Smith, FC1c. I was at breakfast when a tall, ugly guy came into our compartment and literally growled, "Where's Maarr?" He scared the hell out of me and was to be a source of frustration and anger until I finally realized what his real problem was. He would tell me to do something and not be very clear about exactly what to do or how to do it. When we were working on a gun at sea, he handed me a wire with an alligator clip on both ends and told me to go down into the engine room and connect one end to the main switch of the 440-volt generator and the other end to the steel deck. There were two arms on the switch, so I asked which one; he told me to do it, damn it. I did. Whoosh, one clip just about disappeared, all the lights went out, and all power was lost. The loss of power caused problems with the gyro compasses, which didn't please the captain much. All hell broke loose, and I could hear men coming down the ladder to where I was. The hatch slammed open with me behind it, and in complete darkness I sneaked out and up the ladder with the wire in my hand. They never did find out what caused the power failure. Smitty never mentioned it again either. He was always screaming at me, but in the meantime I was studying the manuals during every spare moment and trying not to get in trouble by getting angry.

In a few months I found that many difficulties occurred because Smitty didn't know what he was doing. He never studied to keep up with the new equipment that was starting to arrive, and he had forgotten what he had learned fifteen years ago. Soon he pretty much let me do everything, but he was on my back all the time. His real problem was that he was always in trouble. Every time he went ashore he got drunk, came back to the ship late, and was put on report.

The more I learned, the less he bothered me, except for the amount of work he demanded. It all came to an end just before Pearl Harbor. We had liberty on the Atlantic side of the canal, and Smitty didn't come back. He didn't show up the next day either, so now he was AWOL. The following day we went through the Canal to Balboa, Panama. It was a hot, slow trip, so we always rigged double awnings above the main deck to try and cool down the living spaces. We were almost through the Canal when someone noticed a bulge in the awning. He climbed up to see what it was and found Smitty in a pool of sweat. He was pulled out, hosed down, and put in his bunk. Shortly after our arrival, he was given a summary court-martial and sentenced to time in the brig to be followed by dismissal from the service. Smitty had only about three months to go for twenty years and a pension. I went to visit him in the brig and actually was sorry to see him sitting behind bars, looking so sad and haggard. He asked me if I would bring him a bucket, towel, soap and shaving gear so he could clean himself up. As I was leaving the cell he called, "Hey kid, do you have any Bay Rum?" We had just returned from Kingston, Jamaica, where everyone purchased some because it was so inexpensive. I took the bucket of stuff to him, and as soon as the guard left he took the bottle of Bay Rum out and drank it all. That was the last I saw of Smitty.

The rest of the year was exciting for me. I enjoyed the work and learning how to be a sailor. We were at sea most of the time with drills, drills, and more drills. We had battle stations, work stations, fire stations, watch stations, and abandon ship stations. Except for the work and watch stations, we practiced until we could do everything with our eyes closed. There were a few glitches, however. For my fire station I had been assigned to wear an asbestos suit, and at the first fire drill there was a slight problem. BONG, BONG, BONG! "Fire in the paint locker." The paint locker was in the bow, and access to it was through a circular hatch and down a vertical ladder. I ran to the chest, put on the suit, and started for the locker, which was about one hundred feet away. Boom, I went down on my face and then struggled to get up and get to the "fire." The suit was so big that I was walking on the knees of it, and the glass plate was down below my eyes. Not being able to see or walk very well, I stumbled and bumped along until I reached the hatch. Dick Wenz (six foot, plus) was already down below with his fire extinguisher and, seeing me all tangled

USS *Borie* leads in a high speed turn. We occasionally had maneuvering drills with other destroyers which was fun to watch but was done more to train the deck officers than the enlisted men.

up in the ladder, he reached up and lifted me down. I couldn't have saved myself, never mind rescue someone. From then on I carried the extinguisher and a bigger guy wore the suit.

I was learning fire-control electronics, optics, gyro principles, instrument repair, and the mathematics necessary to align the big guns so that when they were fired, all the projectiles would hit the same spot. I soon knew that I never would go back to being an office clerk. I also found out why Smitty had had so much trouble. With the rapid expansion and modernization of the navy (radar, for example), I had to study all the time to keep up with the new equipment. I never saw Smitty read anything but a comic book.

The most exciting thing was gunnery practice, which was the culmination of a fire-controlman's work. When we boarded the ship, everything, including the fire-control equipment, was in bad shape. Because of a very low budget during the Depression, the big guns had rarely been fired. We had a monumental task ahead of us. I got caught up in the challenge, and in time, the work was done. All the telescopes were aligned. All the firing circuits worked. All the many instruments had been tested and repaired. All the big guns had been adjusted so that when the fire-control director was aimed, the projectiles all hit at the same place. I was the director operator, and when I moved the director onto the target, the guns followed and pointed at the target. When I pulled the trigger at the director, all three of the guns fired at once.

We finally went out for our first competitive gunnery practice with two other ships of our squadron. A destroyer towed a large target about five miles away at a speed of fifteen knots. We were to perform certain maneuvers before firing, and all the while I was to keep the director aimed on the target. At the order to fire, I squeezed the trigger. KAPOW! All the guns blasted. We received the signal from the towing ship: BULL'S-EYE! We fired twenty times, and each time I would say, "Cheeze, I did that." We made twenty bull's-eyes and sailed into port flying an old broom from the top of the mainmast, indicating a clean sweep. I never tired of gunnery practice even though it meant a lot more work for me.

Of course, military duties didn't occupy all our time. There was time to find good friends, a time to explore new places, and, for most of us, a time to be free of our parents. Off duty, we did what we wished without worrying about parental approval, which I had done even though I was twenty years old. That wasn't good for some, but it was good for me.

On a ship the size of a destroyer, you soon get to know everyone, but you become good friends with only a few. Each friend determined how liberty (day ashore) was likely to be spent. Mousey Moultrop was a movie, dinner, or sightseeing type of guy. Jim Allegri, Eddie Johnson, and Ed Malaney were dinner or drinking buddies. Stan Hull fit into the latter category, but not as often as the others. I spent more time with him while at sea, talking seriously about our hopes and dreams. He still is a good friend. I still consider among my best friends Jim Allegri, Mousey, and Bill Schmalberger, although I didn't go ashore with Bill much in those days.

Liberty was almost always the same. We would have dinner and go to a bar or, sometimes, a nice cocktail lounge. Women didn't enter the picture much for most of us except in Brazil, Puerto Rico, and occasionally, Guantanamo City. There was little, if any, social life as we knew it at home. The only women who could be approached were Panamanian natives and not exactly the kind you would take to the office Christmas party. Surprisingly, however, quite a few guys did "shack up" with native girls, paying their living expenses. Often those girls also lived with a guy from the alternate division. When one "sap" was on patrol, the other would be on liberty. You can imagine the incidents that occurred with such a setup.

In Panama City there was a section called the Limits that had several bars with live bands and dance partners. These girls were descendants of the early Spaniards and the native Indians and were about the color of an American girl with a nice Florida tan. The longer we stayed there, the prettier they became! They called these girls "B-Girls" (I don't know why), and they would dance with the servicemen if they were provided with drinks from the bar. Maybe that's how the term "B-Girl" originated. The drinks were colored water for the price of a regular drink. I didn't know how to dance, but it was fun to go to those places because they were like a scene from a 1940 movie: beaded rope curtains, native bands playing Latin music, dark smokey rooms, and dark, sexy, short-skirted women slithering about with sailors. We almost expected to see Humphrey Bogart emerge from a back office.

Our favorite place, the Milwaukee, was clean, sold beer from Milwaukee, and was the nicest place for a cheap liberty. You entered through a wide open door, into a large, brightly lit, white marble-floored room with about twenty white, round tables, all occupied by servicemen.

The large white room was a combination restaurant-bar where we could get hamburgers or just sit around gabbing while we had a few drinks without being bothered by the B-Girls. Once we passed through the beaded curtain and entered the dance hall, we were constantly being asked, "Buy me a drink, sailor?" The drinks were cheap, so I found it easy to pick a girl who seemed nice, sit down, and practice my Spanish. Mostly, however, we stayed in the first room until it was time to go back to the ship.

By the end of the summer of 1941, I was FC3c and had my own striker, Jim Allegri. He was always fun, and we were constant companions ashore. Later I was to get another striker who was a hard worker, Cliff Oxland. The three of us got the equipment in better shape than it had

The Limits, with (left to right) me, Jim Allegri, and Walter Kurz.

ever been. It was the same throughout the ship; without realizing it, we had turned into a fighting unit that enjoyed life on shore and did its job while at sea.

Although we (the crew) still didn't think of a war with Japan, our navy was getting involved in the Atlantic by supplying cover for convoys and, after some sinkings by German U-boats, by arming merchant ships. We did some convoy duty with British ships, but most of the time we were on "neutrality patrol" on both sides of the Panama Canal. Before we finally left Panama I had been through the canal twenty-three times and crossed the isthmus once by train.

Right up until Pearl Harbor, Japanese ships streamed through the canal, carrying mostly scrap iron that was to be returned to us soon in the form of bombs and bullets. Whenever possible, a destroyer went through the locks alongside the Japanese ship, for security, we later learned. Looking back, I wonder what we would or could have done if they had decided to sabotage the locks.

My first view of the Panama Canal was disappointing. I pictured it as it looked in the geography books, not realizing those pictures had been taken when it opened in 1920. Instead of beautiful white concrete, brightly painted "donkeys" (engines that pulled the ships), and waving palm trees, we saw stained walls, rusted engines, and filthy water, contaminated with just about everything. Nevertheless, going through "the Ditch" was at first exciting and, later, always interesting. Incidentally, digging the canal was equal to digging a trench ten feet deep by fifty-five feet wide from California to New York if you base it on the amount of earth removed, which is why, at the time, it was called "the eighth wonder of the world."

Before Pearl Harbor it took us six to ten hours to complete the passage from one ocean to the other, and "special sea detail" was maintained for the whole trip. Special sea detail was a term used for our duties whenever lines (ropes) were involved. This happened when we docked, left the dock, refueled at sea, or passed through the canal. My special sea detail was phone talker on the bow where I passed on orders to the line handlers, forward.

While going through the twelve locks, we were all very busy with the line handling, so I had to stand in the center of the deck with uncomfortable earphones and shout things like "Let go one," or "Haul in two." But for the life of me I don't understand why for the rest of the forty-four-mile trip I had to keep the phones on and remain at my post, all alone. It was a beautiful trip through a jungle mountain paradise and across the largest man-made lake in the world, but after a while it did get tiring.

On one such trip, after clearing the locks I sat down with my back against a hatch, facing toward the stern, prepared for a few hours of watching the scenery go by. Some time later, cruising along nicely, I heard, "Toot, toot," then "toot," several times. A mess attendant (officer's waiter) came out of the hatch carrying a large tray loaded with dirty dishes. He looked back toward me and instantly threw the tray down while running like hell aft and through a door. While I wondered what was bothering him, a CPO came out of the hatch, looked back, and took off, losing his hat over the side. I got up, turned around, and saw an old banana boat, about fifty feet high, bearing down on us, only a short time away from ramming into us. Craning my head almost straight up, in awe at the size of the ship, I decided that I had to get the hell out of there too. I started to run and damn near had my head torn off; I had forgotten to remove my headphones. It did hit us, but only a glancing blow because the captain, seeing that a collision was inevitable, forcibly took control from the professional pilot and altered our course. It's a good thing he did, because if he hadn't we would probably have lost our bow. I wonder if that pilot kept his job.

One of our duties was to patrol the entrances to the canal on both sides and to keep merchant vessels from straying into the minefields that protected those entrances. We had several incidents, but one funny one involved an Italian ship. While we were anchored just outside the minefield on the Atlantic side, we saw a ship heading directly into the mines. Signaling by light, we told them to change course. They signaled back by light, but their signals made no sense so we sent another message to back off. Seeing that they maintained the same course and speed, we fired a shell across their bow, seeing the splash just in front of them. One could almost hear the screeching of brakes as they put their engines in reverse. Their follow-on signals suddenly began to make more sense.

We sometimes anchored alongside the minefields for a week or so and then were relieved by another destroyer from the division. During one such week, a terrible storm arose with high winds and turbulent seas. Captain Miller was ashore, and Ensign Jones (not his real name) was officer of the deck (OD). A message came into the living quarters for the boatswain of the watch (Oakley Hamilton) to report to Mr. Jones. Oakley soon came into the compartment, steaming. Mr. Jones had ordered him to remove the pelican hook (so called because of its shape) that secured the anchor chain in place. This was done so the chain wouldn't be lost as the ship was thrown about by the waves. When Oakley suggested that the hook shouldn't be removed, Jones told him that, damn it, he was the OD, and that was a direct order.

The whole forward crew compartment followed Oakley up the ladder and out onto the windswept deck. Rain or no rain, we didn't want to miss this. Standing as far away as possible, Oakley swung a sledgehammer and knocked out the holding pin, at the same time jumping back out of the way. Rattle, bang, rattle, bang, with a roar of iron upon iron, many fathoms of chain and an anchor were lost, and we couldn't stop laughing at the look on Mr. Jones's face. Ensign Jones was to be involved in several such incidents before he was transferred to patrol boats. After the war I found out that he finally became commanding officer of a destroyer escort (DE).

In late spring and summer of 1941, we stayed at sea longer and longer, first patrolling out in the Pacific and then through the canal to patrol the Atlantic. Although they never told us, it looked as though the Navy Department had an idea that something might happen soon.

In mid-August 1941, we headed south on patrol off the coast of western South America. Soon messages from King Neptune started to appear on the ship's bulletin board indicating that we were going to cross the equator and we should beware of the consequences. From the tone of the messages, which became more alarming as we came closer to the equator, we decided we were going to get our butts kicked when we crossed zero latitude.

As most seafaring sailors know, people who have crossed the line get to initiate those who haven't. What most don't realize is how serious and intense a warship (especially a destroyer) initiation is. The bulletin board messages continued for days, and watching old hands prepare didn't help much. For example, why were so many of them making paddles that were about one foot square and filled with holes? What were the concoctions being mixed by laughing groups and why had we never seen them do that before? Those and other strange activities went on for days, but we who had never been across the equator never could find out what was in store for us. I think the Manhattan Project learned about secrecy from those conspirators.

While those preparations were under way, we continued on our patrol, but the mood was still, "Hell, it ain't our war." I was on an afternoon watch in the crow's nest, and as usual I had a rating study manual with me, which I always hid under my jumper. I would sweep the horizon, study for a while, sweep the horizon, study, and so on. Looking up from one of my study periods, I couldn't believe what I saw. We were heading into a bunch of what looked like telephone poles, about fifty feet long by eight to twelve inches in diameter. I looked down and saw one coming up on our bow. I called down, "Log off the port bow." The captain called, "How far away?" As we heard or more likely felt, I answered, "We just passed it, sir." He asked, "Who's on watch up there?"

"Maher Sir." "Jesus Christ." You see, as I said, it's surprising how many times I was taken to be a religious person. Fortunately, no damage was done to the screws by those logs or I wouldn't have gone to church for a long time.

Because we were heading for the equator, the weather should be getting warmer, right? Wrong! In the rest of the world, yes. Where we were, no. Most of us didn't know that, however, so it came as a shock to wake up and find that we needed jackets on deck.

Everyone knows about the Gulf Stream, and those who have taken cruises to the Caribbean know the wonderful feeling of passing onto its warm waters, especially in the wintertime. In our present position we came into the Gulf Stream's exact counterpart. At our latitude and longitude we entered the Humboldt Current, a cold ocean current coming from the South Pacific, flowing north off South America, along the northern coast of Chile and Peru to southern Ecuador. The water temperature was in the fifties, and air temperature was in the sixties just north of the equator. The area was an interesting study in nature, especially for us city boys. Some of the time we were just off the western coast of South America, close enough to see the Andes Mountains with their snow-covered peaks. Only those particular peaks weren't covered with snow; they were covered with bird droppings. That huge supply of bird dung, called guano, was the backbone of the fertilizer business at that time. We soon found out where it came from and why there was so much of it.

The decks were washed down early in the morning and shortly after came the birds. For the first time we saw condors, huge birds with wingspreads of six to ten feet, that looked like and flew like B-29 bombers. I swear they actually made planned bombing runs with unbelievable precision. They came in one at a time from the stern toward the bow, starting to let go just as they passed over the screws and ending the attack as they were passing over the bridge. Brrrrt, a streak of "snow" was put down from one end of the ship to the other, and before long the ship looked like the snow-covered Andes, only we couldn't sell ours.

We headed west again toward the Galapagos Islands, a chain west of and owned by Ecuador. These islands are now a popular vacation spot and nature-study haven, but when we went there they were, for the most part, uninhabited. As we approached, we saw huge turtles, lots of them, up to five feet in diameter. They swam merrily along without any fear of our ship. Schools of porpoises also swam and played alongside the ship, keeping up with us for miles at speeds of twenty knots. Most interesting, however, were the islands themselves. We maneuvered very close to the beach and anchored near enough to see the penguins and their antics. It was hilarious to see those headwaiters strutting about the beach, falling off the rocks, and in general showing off. A boat was sent ashore, but I wasn't fortunate enough to get to go. Even though the sailors weren't dressed in tuxedos, the penguins allowed them to roam freely among the flock, or whatever a bunch of penguins is called.

We were told that in the days of sailing vessels, a barrel was in place on the islands for exchanging mail. A ship that had just sailed around Cape Horn bound for the western Pacific would drop off mail to be picked up by a ship headed back to the Atlantic.

All that nature study was going on just before or after we crossed the equator. Festivities started on the night of September 3, 1941. We "polliwogs" received threats and promises of doom, both verbally and written by way of the bulletin board. If you look up the definition, you'll find that a polliwog is an immature toad, which will give you some idea of the esteem we were held in by the rest of the crew.

Early Thursday morning, September 4, 1941, the Royal Party arrived from out of the deep. The party consisted of King Neptune, the Royal Princess, the Royal Barber, the Royal Executioner, the Royal Prosecutor, the Royal Scribe (also defense lawyer), the Royal Guard and his deputies, the Royal Polar Bears, and sundry other people whose main object for the day was to devise various methods of torture.

A royal court was set up so King Neptune and the Royal Princess could watch the torture and, at the same time, make sure it was arduous enough. The Royal Guard assigned one of his deputies to each of us so we all had personal attention throughout the initiation. Our guards herded us into a line from the bow all the way back to the stern, occasionally using those paddles across our butts if we didn't move fast enough. Also, they would whack us if we couldn't answer the question, "What are you?" The

Some members of the Royal Court. At center are the Royal Princess (Moultrop) and King Neptune. At right, with the high hat, is Royal Barber Ed Robertson.

answer was "Polliwog," but how the hell could we know? Nobody told us we were polliwogs, and none of us knew that vital fact. As the torture progressed, that question was asked more and more to make sure each guy got in his licks.

We crossed the equator for the first time at longitude 85 degrees, 50 minutes, and 05 seconds, west latitude. As the ship approached the "line," the first man, on the bow, reached down with a boat hook to catch the "line." He pulled it up and passed it to the man behind him, who in turn passed it on to the next man, until the ship had crossed the line without breaking it. Of course we got a few whacks if it looked like we were going to drop it, and it seemed to me that almost all of us were clumsy during that sensitive operation.

With the equator behind us and still intact, we were brought before the Royal Court for trial on the charge of "not being worthy of learning about the SOLEMN MYSTERIES OF THE ANCIENT ORDER OF THE DEEP." Of course we had The Royal Scribe to "defend" us, but somehow or another I had the feeling that, besides being a nut, he was one of "them." At any rate, we were all found guilty, and our punishment began.

I can't remember all the devilish ideas that emerged, but I do recall some of the highlights. While we waited for our turn to receive the standard sentence, any member of the court could do to us or order us to do whatever he wanted. We endured such punishments as having our chests painted, being whacked across our bottoms while we sang a song, wearing a special uniform, or eating raw fish. The only way we could be spared was by answering the by now old question, "What are you?" We answered with any derogatory name we could think of, but none of us, as yet, knew the correct answer.

The first stop was at the Royal Barber, whose chair happened to be wired by the Royal Electrician to an instrument that could make our hair stand up and produce unpleasant tingles throughout our bodies as the Royal Barber gave us the haircut of his choice: a two-inch strip from front to back, a two-inch strip from side to side, both two-inch strips, or a complete shearing, which is what I received.

Next came the push-the-pea-with-your-nose game. It began with a long strip of canvas coated with heavy grease. A dry navy bean was placed at the very end, and we were required to push it to the opposite end, twelve feet away, with our noses, while guys on both sides paddled us.

From that delightful game we went through a gamut of taunting, paddle-swinging sailors and headed straight for the torpedo tubes, in particular the tube from which the eighteen-inch torpedo had been removed. The tube was only about shoulder width, and the inside was coated with heavy grease. I was told to crawl through, so I started in with my arms to my sides for pushing. You can imagine what a slow-moving, well-set-up target my fanny made for the ever-present paddle wielders. It wasn't easy to get through, but my head finally emerged at the opposite end. A man was there to greet me, and as he smiled into my face he said, "Oh, you've had enough." At the same time he sprayed a cool liquid into my face. Thinking it was water, I turned my head in all directions to take advantage of the delightful turn of events. Later I was to find that the liquid was penetrating oil, and I would have a bloodshot eye for the rest of my life.

As I pulled myself out of the tube by grabbing whatever was near, I heard the word "polliwog" whispered. THAT's IT! I was led to a canvas pool that had been constructed on deck, with a greased slide that came down from the afterdeckhouse into the center of the pool. In the pool, stripped to the waist, were four or five of the huskiest, toughest men on the ship. I

The Royal Bears—smiles like pussy cats, but these husky Bears played their role with relish.

was placed on the slide head first, on my back and pushed, zip, down into the water and into arms of the Royal Bears. They threw me back and forth and ducked me under, all the while asking, "What are you?" I, now knowing the word, replied, "Polliwog." That was no longer the correct answer. I don't remember how I found out before I was drowned, but at some time I gave the name of my new status, "shellback," and now I was a full-fledged shellback. Shellback originally was the term used for an old sailor, hardened by experience.

I was to cross the equator nine more times, so I got my licks in as a member of the Royal Party more than enough to make up for the pain and suffering I had encountered. To tell the truth, in spite of how silly the whole thing may sound, it was one more lifetime experience that I wouldn't have missed for the world.

In October 1941, we received two Venezuelan naval officers aboard for training, Lieutenant Fortoul and Ensign Mirabal. It seems that Fortoul was very wealthy and had given his large yacht to his government to be used as a subchaser, and they, in turn, had made him its captain. Ensign Mirabal was also to be an officer aboard the subchaser.

Borie sailors in the Villa Lobos Bar.

Ensign Arnold and I were the only two men who stood regular bridge watches and also spoke Spanish. So Mirabal stood the same watches as I did, while Fortoul stood duty with Arnold. This arrangement allowed me to practice my high school Spanish, and it improved greatly.

Most of us liked liberty in Panama City on the Pacific side of the canal better than in Colón on the Atlantic side. I know I did—Panama City had more nice shops and restaurants.

In particular, I can recall two beautiful nightclub-style restaurants that had live music. Most Panamanians couldn't afford to go to those places, but they were usually crowded with Canal Zone workers, the military, and local successful businessmen. The Atlas Gardens and El Rancho were places we went when we wanted a nice evening as near to home style as possible. Both had first-class dinners and good orchestras that played the big band music of the time. Allegri and I spent many enjoyable evenings at both those night spots.

While based in Panama we didn't always go into town on our liberty days. Both sides of the canal had navy post exchanges with places to eat, drink beer, or go to a movie. The prices were much better there, so if we were low on funds or just lazy, that's where we spent our time.

We were stationed for so long in Panama that after a while boredom set in. If anyone thought of something different to do, we jumped at the opportunity. One such occasion was a trip into the "jungle." I don't know

Clinkenbeard and Sherman at Villa Lobos Bar. The guys are starting to look like recruiting posters!

who arranged the trip or how we got there, but the place was unique. We went to a town called Las Arraijas and hit the first (and only) bar we found. Our gang spent almost a full day there, and we were the only customers.

We had been at the bar only a short time when the bartender asked a group of us to come with him through a small door alongside the bar. When we were inside, he pointed at a disheveled sailor stretched out on the floor. He was obviously unconscious because of booze. We were told that he had been there many days and was now in deep trouble. It seems he was one of those guys, a radioman, who had set up a girl with an apartment and had arrived home a day early. He found his girl in bed with a sailor from another ship, who happened to be a good friend of his. The radioman had been in love with the girl, and seeing her in bed with another man crushed him. We decided he was in so much trouble already that it would be better if he was allowed to make his own decisions. Being AWOL that long was bad news.

In early December we were off on patrol in the Pacific again—normal, boring patrol. Hell, it ain't our war. It came as a complete shock when we received the news of Pearl Harbor while on that patrol, only a few hours from Balboa, Panama. The Japanese wouldn't dare! But they did.

As we approached the dock, almost everyone's attention was on a beautiful woman who was apparently waiting for the *Borie*. (She turned out to be the wife of one of our officers, and she had decided to move to Panama.) Some of us, however, were more interested in getting our mail and news about how the war was going. The next day all dependents who had been living in the Canal Zone, including the beautiful wife who had just arrived, were sent back home.

Even when we learned of the great amount of damage to our fleet, we were saying things like, "It won't last six months," or "Their airplanes were made of plywood." As it happened, their fighter planes were much better than ours for a long time, and it was to be almost a year before our fleet was strong enough to take the war to them. By pure chance our carriers weren't at Pearl Harbor, although some of them were supposed to be, and they were able to hold the line until we were stronger. In fact, although we didn't know it then, the battle of Midway in June 1942 was the turning point in the war against Japan. That infamous engagement and the earlier battle of the Coral Sea were the first sea battles in history to be decided entirely by combat with airplanes.

The two Venezuelan officers were detached from the ship, and I knew that I would miss Ensign Mirabal. The commander of Destroyer Division 67 (our division) came aboard, making the *Borie* his flagship.

We refueled and restocked provisions. We were ready to head back out to sea in six hours, and we left at 2025. Higher authority was worried that the Japanese might be preparing to attack the canal, so a battle line was set up from northern South America to southern California, but nothing ever developed. It was not actually a battle line but an area, called the Panama Sea Frontier, that had recently been established to protect the Panama Canal. The frontier covered a large area on both sides of the canal that was to be patrolled by a small number of ships, including ours.

I think the Japanese goofed. If they had damaged just one set of locks, they would have delayed our transfer of ships from the Atlantic to the Pacific to such an extent that they might have been able to achieve most of their objectives. For example, the turning point for United States ground troops (marines) was in August 1942 with the battle for Guadalcanal, a battle that prevented the Japanese from building an airstrip there. That battle would not have been possible if the Panama Canal had been closed early in the war. I think it would have been possible for Japan to do that if it wanted to accept the losses involved.

We were on our first wartime patrol, but none of us really felt as if we were in a war. It was someone's dream. Captain Miller came out of his cabin early on December 8, and as was his usual custom, he went to the side of the bridge and stretched while looking around the horizon. He looked, shouted, "General quarters!" and ran for a pair of binoculars. A seaplane on the horizon was circling around and around. None of our lookouts had seen it, even though it was our war now.

The plane disappeared over the horizon, and Captain Miller called all hands not on watch to assemble on the forecastle, leaving command of the ship to our squadron commander whose quarters were aboard our ship. When we were assembled (over two-thirds of the crew) on deck, he gave us a pep talk about doing our jobs right if we wanted to make it through the war alive. While he was talking, a shout came from the squadron commander, "Pete, for Christ's sake, look out forward!" We all looked forward and saw a spread of torpedoes heading directly at our bow. General quarters sounded as Captain (Pete) Miller shouted to the bridge, "Hard right!"

What followed could have been taken from a Keystone Cops movie, except it wasn't really funny. During our training to get to our battle stations as quickly as possible and avoid congestion, all hands went forward on the starboard side and aft on the port side. This set up one-way traffic through the narrow doors. More than one hundred men now tried to go aft through one door. What a mess. But the captain's command to change course had done the trick because as we turned sharply to the starboard, the torpedo spread, if indeed they were torpedoes, turned to our port. We all learned in less than a week that we weren't playing a game, and if we wanted to stay alive we had better stay alert. In fact, for the first time, I had the thought that a guy could get hurt out here.

On December 8 we also started steering zigzag courses while on the 2000 to 2400 watch. A zigzag course made it more difficult for subs to anticipate our future position and thus more difficult to set their torpedoes. When you came on watch, the man you relieved would tell you what the present course was and show you where you were on the course-change list. The list gave time of day and course for that time (for example: 10:00—000, 10:05—090, 10:13—010, and so on). The time on any one course was never long enough to give a sub time to get a fix on our position.

At 2100 we received our first sound contact report from our sonar operator. Boing, Boing, Boing! GENERAL QUARTERS! The port engine was stopped, and the starboard engine went to full speed. Add an order, "Hard left rudder," and it made for one hard change of course. I even gave myself a "Jesus Christ" that time.

We made many changes of course and speed while Captain Miller set up a search pattern. After finding nothing by 2135, we secured from general quarters and resumed our normal patrol course and speed.

We did many stupid things in those early days. On December 10 we started to "clear the ship." First we dumped a load of books. After that we jettisoned all floating material and anything else that was included in the "clear the ship bill." I guess that was to make the ship safer in case of battle. Among the stuff dumped was a wooden grate from the deck of the flying bridge, all the bridge windows, and all our paint.

At the first general quarters drill, we discovered that I couldn't reach the telescope, so I couldn't see to fire the guns. We hit a bad storm on the patrol, and the bridge was soaked by the sea and the rain. When we got into port we received orders to paint the ship at once. Time was lost while we waited for new paint to arrive.

Remaining on patrol, we continued our drills. On December 11, at 1215, we had another submarine scare. Someone reported a torpedo wake, so we went to general quarters. I think by now we had some jumpy sailors and what the watch had seen was porpoise wakes.

Also on December 11 we were to find out what kind of CO Captain Miller was. We were "hot to trot" even though Captain Miller had informed us that, as destroyer men, we were expendable.

We were heading west, out into the Pacific and approaching a large rain squall, when suddenly a large ship appeared out of the dark cloud. Was it a Japanese battleship? The captain ordered, "All hands, battle stations; all engines ahead full; stand by for a torpedo attack." As we raced directly toward the much larger ship, which had more and larger guns, a flashing signal appeared from its bridge. It was one of our cruisers, the USS *Trenton,* but Captain Miller hadn't known that when we started our turn toward the *Trenton* and prepared for a torpedo attack.

On Saturday, December 13, we intercepted a ship and sent a boarding party. It turned out to be a "huge" fishing vessel of 175 tons, the SS *California*. As you can see, we weren't jumpy at all. Not much we weren't.

On December 11, we docked alongside a pier in Balboa, took on stores and fuel, and again headed out to sea in the Pacific. We patrolled to the southern end of the Panama Sea Frontier, arriving in the vicinity of the Galapagos Islands on December 16, where we patrolled around the various islands until anchoring at midnight. We arrived back at Balboa on

December 22 and spent Christmas Eve and Christmas Day alongside the dock. I remember being on watch with Mousey on Christmas Eve, toasting each other with small cans of tangerine juice. That was one of five Christmas Eves we spent away from home. Walter Kurz and I had shore patrol in Panama City the day after Christmas. It could have been worse—like Christmas Day.

For a change we went to sea again on December 27, to patrol the southern part of the frontier, arriving at the Galapagos Islands at 2106 on December 30. Early on that patrol we were ordered to search for one of our planes that had gone down. We searched and searched for days and saw nothing. The captain finally said that if we didn't find it by sundown on January 16, we would call off the search. In the late afternoon, Ensign Young asked for permission to go up in the crow's nest to search. We all wondered that if the regular lookouts couldn't find it, what did he think he was going to do?

A little time later, a cry came from above: "Object on the horizon, off the port bow." Ensign Young had spotted the plane! It was one of the few things that had gone right—and a very good thing for the fliers because we were about to abandon the search.

We picked up speed and steamed over to the wreckage to find the crew of four sitting on the wings, waving and cheering. They had survived on emergency rations and, except for sunburn, were in pretty good shape. They had run out of water, however, so they would soon have been in real trouble.

At first we tried to save the plane by towing, but we broke the tow line. It was decided that the plane should be sunk because it was a navigational hazard. Our four-inch guns were loaded and fired one shot at a time. We either missed or made small holes that didn't accomplish much, which really annoyed Captain Miller. In fact, at one time he broke out a .30 caliber rifle, and we heard, "BOOM, CRACK," but the plane kept floating serenely along.

Captain Miller, sitting in the captain's chair on the bridge, said, "Maher, sink that airplane." Hot damn! I headed the ship's bow for the floating wreckage and went right through it. How many guys can say they put a bomber plane (a PBY) down with a destroyer?

While we fiddled around with the PBY, we were traveling in the general direction of Balboa. We entered the channel for Balboa at 0659 on January 23, but we didn't go into Balboa. Instead, we kept right on going toward the canal entrance, entering the first set of locks at 0800. I was about to spend a long day sitting on my duff on the steel deck while we made a northerly transit of the Panama Canal.

After tying up at a pier in the Coco Solo Naval Base at 1421 (the Atlantic side of the canal), we took on a small amount of food and headed right back through the canal for the Pacific side. The business of transit canal, patrol, transit canal, patrol, and so on was to go on for quite a while, and the situation really was like someone said: "It is the war and war is hell." For us it wasn't hell, but it sure as hell was boring.

We entered dry dock at Balboa Naval Base on February 16, 1942. This was the second time we Jersey sailors entered dry dock. A huge quantity of barnacles can adhere to the hull of a ship in a relatively short time. Those crustaceans cut down the speed of a destroyer by about five knots, and now that we were at war, we wanted all the speed we could get. Barnacles must be removed while they're still wet and soft; if left to dry, they turn into a cementlike substance that has to be chipped off with hammer and chisel.

The first time we entered dry dock, before the water was pumped out of the dock, all hands were put over the side on stages (scaffolds), with long-handled ice scrapers. We lowered ourselves to water level so we could remove the barnacles as the water went down. That method didn't work well for us civilian sailors. It was much harder work than we had anticipated. We really had to push hard to get the stuff off. That in itself wasn't too bad, but each time we pushed, the stage moved out from under us. Each push almost dumped us into the receding water. The water went down much faster than we could remove the barnacles. The navy learned a lesson, and the second time we entered the dock, large groups of natives, holding scrapers, waited on floating platforms. As soon as we were in place, the platforms were aligned around the ship, and the glop was removed as fast as the water went down.

During this period I spent one evening talking to the chief boatswain's mate, Chief Brown. He told me that he hated being in this particular dry dock because he had been here before. That time he came back from liberty on his motorcycle (drunk as a skunk) and drove it right over the edge of the dock, falling to the concrete bottom about 50 feet below. Although hospitalized, he came out of it without any serious injuries, but he was now afraid that something might happen again. Of course I told him that the odds of that happening again were ridiculous and, besides, this time he didn't have a motorcycle. One morning as I was washing up, a man shaving next to me asked, "Did you hear what happened to Chief

Brown last night?" He came back from liberty, drunk, and fell off the gangway (a narrow plank with a rope guard), landing on his head on the bottom of the dry dock. This time he was killed.

Now we had to do over some of the dumb things we had changed during those first days of the war. Portholes were put on the front of the bridge, replacing the windows that we had thrown over the side; a new platform was put on the flying bridge so we could use the gun director; and we had to paint the ship with a camouflage pattern. We stayed in the yard for about one week getting the ship ready for war again.

Then we were back on two-ocean patrol. Of course, the two oceans were separated by only about fifty miles or so. I guess the authorities were really worried about an attack on the canal from both sides because they sure kept us busy. Any ships that could be spared now started to flow through the isthmus to strengthen the Pacific Fleet.

Even though we realized the importance of our job patrolling the entrance to the canal on both sides, we still hoped orders would come for us to head for the South Pacific to join what was left of the fleet—but no such luck. Except for some small incidents, it turned out to be a boring, tiresome job.

In one period we sailed out into the Pacific, patrolled for three weeks, and came into Panama to find all our supplies on the dock. We loaded up before proceeding through the canal again, with no time ashore. We patrolled the Atlantic for two weeks, then went back to the Pacific for three more weeks, then again out into the Atlantic with no shore leave. Shortly after we hit the open sea, I had the wheel watch (steering the ship) and had orders to steer a zigzag course to the northeast. By now we were very tired. With all the work and watches, we were lucky if we got five hours of sleep a night.

We steered by what was called a gyro repeating compass, an electrical compass that made a ticking sound as the ship changed heading, one tick for each one degree of change. On this particular day, I would rest my head on my arms on top of the helm as soon as I was on the proper heading. If we started to drift off course, I would hear the ticking, correct the heading, and go back to my rest position.

Suddenly I was smashed against the wheel, and I looked up to see the bow with the head of a huge whale (about forty feet long) on the port side and the tail on the starboard side. I looked at the compass and saw that I was eighty degrees off course. I slowly started turning the wheel to ease the ship back on course. Of course, nobody would notice the beautiful pink wake as it arched steeply around. The captain came running out of the chart room, which was a small room on the bridge. He called out, "What's the matter, Maher, did you lose steerage-way?" I answered, "Oh no, sir, it's just time to zig." At the next position check they never could figure out why we were so far away from where we were supposed to be.

As it turned out, that incident made me a hero with the crew. The whale's body had busted our sound dome, a cover that extended below the keel to protect our sound gear. With the sound equipment damaged, our usefulness as a submarine hunter was lost, so we turned around and headed for Panama and, at long last, liberty.

At a later date I had the wheel in the same general area where I had rammed the whale when the cry rang out, "Whale spouts off the starboard beam." We could smell the fish odor of the blow if the wind was right; today it was right, so I did smell the whales. Captain Miller called to the quartermaster of the watch and told him to relieve Maher on the wheel until we got clear of the whales because he didn't trust me.

During those early days of the war, the enemy launched many submarine attacks on the Panama Canal approaches. During one two-week period, with only three U-boats, Germany averaged one sinking a day. We were kept hopping, both on patrols and on convoy duty.

Our duties now consisted of both patrolling the canal approaches and doing convoy duty. Our first convoys were between the Canal Zone and Cuba and between the Canal Zone and Kingston, Jamaica. That duty was not considered a "piece of cake." So many ships were torpedoed in the area that it soon became known as "Torpedo Junction."

Liberty in Cuba while we served under Captain Miller was terrible. We were not allowed off the Guantanamo Bay naval base, which meant only 3.2 percent beer and none of the social life that could be found in civilian bars, restaurants, and clubs. We considered Kingston, Jamaica, a pretty good liberty port. At least the people spoke English. It was the only place we had been in over a year where they did.

When American sailors started to arrive regularly the economy of Kingston changed drastically. We spent money, tipped outrageously, and in general treated the people well. It was to be many years later before the cry, "Yankee go home" was to be heard in Jamaica.

While we longed for liberty in the United States or for that matter any modern city where we could associate with people on our own social level (especially women), this for now was the only game in town.

There were two regrettable results of the influx of people into Jamaica because of the war in Europe:

1. Prostitution became rampant. Young girls found out they could make much more money this way than by carrying bananas or waiting on tables. Boys eight to twelve years old would crowd the area alongside our gangways trying to sell their sisters. They would even grab you by the hand and try to drag you off with them.

2. The Jamaicans became accustomed to a better economy during the period 1939–45 and were not prepared for what was to happen at war's end. Except for bananas, trade dropped to zero and the British gave them their independence, leaving them to shift for themselves. They now became a poverty-ridden country.

Even though ships were going down, we all longed for a transfer to a fighting ship in the South Pacific. All requests for transfer were routinely turned down. Our captain did not want to lose his trained crew, even though many of the new warships were heading west with almost all untrained men.

Captain Miller pulled strings to keep from losing any of his crew. A directive came to all ships from the Navy Department to allow all men above a certain rank, which I was, to apply for duty as naval aviation cadets. Twenty-five of us applied, and we were sent to the Naval Hospital in Panama for our screening physicals. All of us, young and healthy as we were, failed! I failed because of my eyes.

While we were walking around the base waiting for transportation back to the ship, a Jeep went by and the driver started yelling at us. I turned to the fellow I was with, saying, "I don't know him, do you know him?" He said, "I don't know him." The Jeep swung around, screeching, and pulled up alongside us. The driver turned out to be a former classmate of mine from high school. He was a corpsman at the hospital, and when I told him why we were there he asked, "Are you guys from the *Borie?*" When I told him yes, he said, "Hell, we knew about you, and we heard that everyone was going to fail!" Later on, being concerned, I went to a civilian doctor to have my eyes examined, and he told me my eyes were better than 20/20! So much for getting a new ship.

In early May 1942, one of the best things that had happened so far occurred. Lt. Cmdr. Phil Osborn came aboard and relieved Captain Miller as commanding officer. Since the war started we had gotten little rest or recreation. Our morale was starting to sag, not only because of boredom but because we had not touched a United States port in eighteen months and had not had any leave during that time.

Within a few days of Osborn's arrival, we set sail on yet another convoy to Cuba, but this one evolved differently because of Osborn's influence. We herded the convoy into Guantanamo Bay, but we didn't enter. Instead, we headed northwest at about twenty knots. Osborn had managed to arrange a few days of stateside liberty for us!

What a thrill to see home again as we rounded the southern tip of Florida and sailed up the western coast, always keeping land in sight. We entered Tampa Bay about May 20 and headed toward St. Petersburg. Proceeding up a channel to our berthing area, we sailed alongside a beautiful, palm-tree-lined beach on our port side. The beach was crowded with people, and jokingly I said, "They're cheering for us," knowing full well that nobody ever welcomed a naval vessel.

I was wrong again. We dropped anchor in the channel because the docking facilities weren't big enough to handle a destroyer. However, we were close enough to see the cheering crowd on the dock. We were the first fighting ship to enter that port since Pearl Harbor. What a time we were to have—and what a time the people of St. Petersburg were to have.

Dressed in our finest tailor-made whites, wearing our ribbons, and aching to touch American soil again, we went ashore in our motor-driven lifeboats. I'm sure you have all seen movies of sailors coming ashore, standing packed tightly together in the boat and raising hell in anticipation of a great night. We were no different.

Jim Allegri, Mousey, Fred Bartell, and I went ashore in the first boat. As we approached the dock, the sound of cheers and the excitement of our greeters was unbelievable. We didn't feel like heroes, nor were we, but I know now what it feels like to be one. Nothing like that had happened to us before; usually it was just the opposite. By the end of our liberty, I was to know why, and in fact I was to get a hint of why in just a few minutes.

As we jumped out of the rocking boat, the crowd surged toward us, all dressed in their Sunday best. They were so anxious to welcome and entertain us that they grabbed us by the arms and attempted to haul us away to dinner or whatever. I was unfortunate enough to be walking up the dock with Bartell alongside me when we were approached by two pretty young girls who asked if we would like to go home with them for the afternoon and have dinner in the evening. After all the terrible liberties we had had in bars frequented only by dirty natives, that would have made my day. However, Bartell replied with a crude sexual response. I could have fallen through the sidewalk as the girls turned and ran away, probably to fear sailors forever, even civilian ones. I asked him, "Why did you do that?" His answer was that he didn't have all that much time so he didn't want to waste any just fooling around. I told him to go on ahead as I wanted to wait for Jimmy, who was coming up behind us, followed by Jim Aikenhead.

As Jim and I started to walk toward town I saw two motherly looking women approaching. Although I didn't approve of what Bartell had done, an afternoon of tea and crumpets wasn't what I had in mind either. When the women came up to us, one said, "Come along with us, boys; we have a wonderful home-cooked meal all ready for you." I replied, "Thank you, but I have relatives here. Do you see that nice young man behind us? That's all he talked about on the way in here." Good old Jim Aikenhead was too polite to say no, and he was ticked off at me for a long time.

What a time we had, at least for the first couple of days. All those patriotic people just couldn't do enough for us. They invited us to their homes and churches, on picnics, and whatever else they could think of to make us happy. The nicest thing for us was to be able to sit in a lounge or restaurant with clean, shining, pretty, young American girls who were having as much fun as we were. We sang, danced, and laughed, and for a while we forgot the boredom (not the danger) we were soon to go back to. For the first two days the whole town was in a carnival mood, with everyone, young and old, out on the streets sharing our fun, if only by watching.

I had shore patrol on the second night, along with Ed Robertson, and there were no problems until it was time to head back to the ship. We went to one end of town and started our sweep through the bars and restaurants, making sure everyone we saw started back. That was done with a "Let's go, sailor" or "Time to go." An old woman came running up to me saying, "Why are you spoiling their fun? You should be ashamed of yourself." She started to bash at me with an umbrella, and the only thing I could do was run.

Things changed. The men started to do things that were not expected of red-blooded American boys, some funny and some not so funny. One man walked back to the ship in broad daylight, drunk as hell, barefoot, with no hat and two large ducks on leashes. Many innocent young women were insulted by the men, both drunk and sober. The ship received a message that the police were trying to get a man out of a tree. He was drunk and refused to come down, and they didn't want to hurt him. A ship's officer was sent over and ordered him down with the threat of a court-martial. Those ugly things were done by only a few men, but it took only these few to ruin it for all of us. St. Petersburg was happy to see us go, and when we left, except for a few girls who had made friends with some of the crew, there was no cheering crowd to send us off to the wars. I didn't blame them.

With Phil Osborn in command of the ship, morale started upward again. I thought Captain Miller was an excellent officer, and I had trusted him with my life. However, he was a "by the book officer" and didn't worry about things like liberty. Captain Osborn, in addition to being a good officer, was also a very nice guy (he still is, and I still see him occasionally), and he did think quality time ashore was important.

All my life I've been known for doing things with a "seems like a good idea" attitude only to find that I have done something dumb. Maybe the idea really wasn't dumb, it just turned out that way. Such things happened so often where I worked that anything that started out right and ended with a laughable disaster became known as "pulling a Maher."

While we were tied up in Balboa, a large troopship came through the canal and docked. It was the USCG *Wakefield,* formerly the passenger ship SS *Manhattan.* We heard that it was carrying a large contingent of marines from New Jersey. (The *Wakefield* had been bombed by the Japanese in December 1941.) The *Wakefield* was tied up in front of a large building that I went through to get alongside the ship. I scooted through, not paying any attention to people standing around or anything else. This was a big ship with a deck about thirty feet above the dock. There were MPs all up and down the dock, but they didn't pay any attention to me as I called up to the marines who were looking over the side, "Anybody from Kearny, New Jersey?" One guy said, "Yeah, Charlie Fergusen." Charlie had been one of my best friends in high school. I heard the cry, "Hey Charlie," moving along the deck.

Charlie appeared on deck, and we shouted back and forth about old friends. Suddenly Charlie got a great idea. He asked if I would mail a letter for him because they hadn't been allowed to mail any letters before leaving the States. I told him, "Why not?" At once, all the guys wanted to know if I would mail theirs also. Why not?

Charlie appeared with a stack of letters about six inches thick. He hollered, "Here they come," and threw them to me. The dummy had probably put only one elastic band around them because the stack opened up and the letters fell like leaves in a light rain. Most, if not all, fell into the water.

How could I have known that the shipload of marines was a big secret? Whistles started to blow up and down the dock, followed by the hammering of the MPs' boots as they converged in my direction. I might have pulled a Maher now and then, but I had become good at recognizing when it happened and, more important, extricating myself expeditiously. Having been in that building many times, I knew where to go. I hauled ass down the side of the building so I couldn't be cornered, ducked inside before the MPs could see me, and hid. They were sure I wasn't dumb enough to hide in the building.

Shortly after, we departed Balboa escorting the *Wakefield* on its way to New Zealand. We hoped we would go all the way that time, but it was not to be. Moving at twenty-one knots, with motor torpedo boats also as escorts, it was apparent that our fuel wouldn't get us far unless arrangements had been made to rendezvous with a refueling vessel. No such luck. At about the midpoint of our range for that speed, we turned around and, with our tails between our legs, headed back to Panama, arriving on June 2.

We took on fuel and provisions before we made another crossing of the canal. I realized that a canal transit was no longer a glamorous adventure when the native line handlers started calling to me, standing on the bow, "Que habla, Roberto?" It was even worse when I found myself responding, "Como està su esposa, Juan?" (How's your wife, John?)

After a long rest, until noon the next day, we left Cristobal, acting as an escort for Convoy CS-5, consisting of only two British ships, the *Ocean Volunteer* and *War Mama,* at a speed of ten knots. The trip was uneventful, but not without anxiety. We were operating in the area between Cuba and Florida, and that was indeed a Torpedo Junction. At that time in 1942 the U-boats were having a field day. The previous month they had sunk forty-one ships in the small area we were traversing.

We received daily reports of nearby sinkings and attacks. Copies of all those reports were placed on our deck bulletin board, so we were aware of what was happening. But whether by skill or accident, we arrived safely off the coast of Key West. We were relieved of the convoy at sea and proceeded into Key West for fuel.

We had a couple of days of liberty at the Key West Naval Base, but it was hot so sleeping was almost impossible. It would have been completely impossible, but the breeze made by the flapping mosquitoes cooled it off somewhat. Anyway, things were so bad that the captain moved the ship out to an anchorage where it was cooler and there were no mosquitoes. We left the area after two days with an eight-knot convoy of eleven ships for another cruise through Torpedo Junction. We weren't happy about traversing that area in the first place, but an eight-knot convoy made the situation worse. Sure enough, the next day a navy plane circled and indicated that a submarine had been sighted. Since a sub had been reported earlier within five miles of our position, the CO gave orders to attack.

That turned out to be fun. Whoop, whoop, whoop, our horn screamed out. At the same time, flank speed was ordered (as fast as we could go), and as our bow rose like a speedboat, we passed what looked like a troopship with the men on deck cheering and waving. Osborn ordered two depth charges dropped, "just in case." With the horns blowing, the bow crashing through the waves, and depth charges exploding, we must have made an impressive appearance as we went to do battle for our troops. Hell, I was impressed.

A periscope was sighted, and as we headed straight at it we started firing gun no. 1 (four inch). We fired five rounds, but the sub had guts. It never moved. It was a piece of wreckage from a torpedoed steamer. It was all under water, except for an extension that, from a distance, looked exactly like a periscope.

As we passed the troopship to return to our position, we gave the victory sign, which again was to the sound of cheering from the "saved" troops. Oh, what the hell. We gave them a memory that would last a lifetime.

That convoy was a fiasco from the start. Twice at night the navy planes dropped flares, lighting up the convoy and causing the merchant ships to mill around and show lights that said, "Hey Adolf, here we are." Fortunately, no subs were in the area or else they thought, "Nobody is that stupid; this must be a trick."

In early afternoon of June 15 we were ordered to leave the convoy and search for survivors of the USAT *Merrimack,* which had been sunk by *U-107* on the night of June 9.

At about 10:00 P.M. on June 9, the *Merrimack,* en route from New Orleans to the Panama Canal, was struck by a torpedo on the starboard side, just forward of the bridge. Apparently the ship had not been zigzagging, even though it was doing only eleven knots. (In those early days of the war, most of the captains didn't want to zigzag; they wanted to depend on speed.) According to survivors, after it was hit, the ship immediately listed about thirty-five degrees. The explosion knocked out all lights and demolished the starboard lifeboat (no. 1) and the forward life raft. When survivors reached the boat deck they found no. 1 wrecked and no. 2 fully loaded. Those men lowered no. 2 and then attempted to lower rafts. During that time, the engines were still turning full speed ahead, so when the rafts were lowered and cut loose, they drifted far astern. Far worse, the ship's rudder was hard right so that when no. 2 was lowered, it was caught in the propellers and completely demolished. The nine survivors we found had escaped by diving off the starboard side of the stern and swimming to the two rafts on which we later found them.

The *Merrimack* had a navy gun crew of eight men aboard, commanded by Ensign Marshall, who was awarded the Silver Star medal, posthumously, for his bravery during that action. All of the men reported to their stations immediately after the explosion and trained their guns to starboard, all the while searching diligently for a surfaced submarine. When the forward part of the ship was awash, Ensign Marshall gave orders to abandon ship. Only one gun crew member survived, John J. Waller, seaman second class.

All members of the crew had police whistles that could be heard from all directions, but in darkness the men could not be located, and the rafts finally drifted away. The men on rafts listened as the sounds gradually died.

The nine survivors spent the next six days drifting under a burning sun, carefully rationing their food and water. Several United States planes flew close without seeing them, and once a destroyer passed close by, but they were evidently too far away. Some of the men became disheartened and began to swim near the raft, indifferent to the dangers of sharks.

When we found them, they were in pretty good shape except for being badly sunburned. Their life rafts were huge rectangular things tied together. One of the emergency provisions was a supply of malted milk balls, which looked and tasted like those that are sold today. Now when I say a supply, I mean a *supply*. Every man aboard the *Borie* had malted milk balls coming out of his giggy. That wasn't bad because our ship's store was about as big as a telephone booth. They told us they weren't worried about food (hell, they had enough malted milk balls to feed the Allied invasion forces at Normandy) but they had started to worry about water.

We rejoined the convoy on its southerly course until we broke away from it on June 18, arriving in Panama early in the morning of June 19.

While we were gone in June, eight ships were sunk near the entrance to the canal at Colón. All this damage was done by one submarine, *U-159*. It was kind of funny because my mother always wrote how glad she was that I was in such a "safe" area, only doing guard duty at the Panama Canal.

Because of the Japanese attacks on the Aleutians and Midway during the first week of June, the Panama Sea Frontier had to expect a carrier or submarine raid at Balboa on the Pacific side of the canal. Between the sub threat on the east coast and the Japanese threat on the west coast, we were kept mighty busy.

As it turned out, the east coast was by far the most important area to the war effort and things weren't going well as of June 30, 1942. In spite of my mother's peace of mind that the *Borie* had "safe duty," that was not exactly true. From January 1 through June 30, German subs had sunk 297 ships in our area of operations.

It would be about forty years before we found out just how important our participation in the battle of the Atlantic had been. Military historians were to say that winning that "war" had a greater impact than the attack on Pearl Harbor.

Also, by then reinforcements for the Pacific Fleet were constantly passing through the canal. One such group was a task force consisting of the battleship *North Carolina,* the carrier *Wasp,* cruisers *Quincy* and *San Juan,* and seven destroyers. We were lucky enough to see that force go through, and everyone started to yearn for some real action.

By July 1942 everyone was putting in for transfers to any ship or station, but none was being approved. Bartell, however, managed to get a swap with a gunner's mate on a PT boat. Those were small torpedo boats, very fast and very hard riding, and that gunner wanted to get off because he could no longer stand the pounding. The squadron was practicing its attack technique before it headed out to do battle with the Japanese, and that was good enough for Bartell. We soon heard that Bartell had been awarded the Navy Cross, posthumously. The PT boats burned gasoline at such a rapid rate that they stored drums of fuel in hidden coves so they didn't have to return to base so often. As Bartell's boat went into one of those coves, bow on, it received a fusillade of machine-gun fire from a Japanese force that had discovered their cache. With only the bow gun able to bear, Bartell jumped into the hail of bullets and commenced firing the twenty-millimeter machine gun and continued to do so, even though mortally wounded, until all the enemy were dead. He may have been a reprobate while drunk, but he was a brave young man when it counted.

On July 3 we departed Cristobal (Atlantic side of the Canal Zone) with orders to intercept and escort a convoy to Kingston, Jamaica. We liked Kingston for liberty better than we did Cristobal. Of course, that was like comparing a headache to an ulcer.

While in Kingston, I visited my cousin on the destroyer *Duncan* and tried to arrange a transfer to it, but of course that didn't work out. For the second time, and not the last, a ship I tried to get on was to be sunk. The *Duncan* was to go down off Guadalcanal before the end of the year.

The *Borie* and the *Duncan* left Kingston, escorting a small convoy to Cuba. It was an uneventful trip, but while we were in Guantanamo an event took place that not only cleared our sinuses but spoiled our day. There was no better place for a submarine to lurk than a harbor where convoys were formed. A small convoy was scheduled to sail, so the *Borie* and the *Barry* were ordered to sortie out ahead of the convoy and drop depth charges to drive any sub down. We dropped seven charges, and they were all duds. We still had only World War I charges, although new ones had been on order for a long time. That would have made me nervous when we roared in to attack a threatening sub contact except that my mother had said I was safe.

Although everyone aboard respected Capt. Phil Osborn as a CO, he soon became a ship's legend and was loved by all the crew. He was a Hollywood skipper, one about whom the ship's crew bragged to other crews. He expected us to perform our duties as they should be done, but he did his best to give us liberty and, more important, quality liberty.

He liked good liberty, too. Many times when we were about to tie up to a dock, Osborn would appear for special sea detail in his dress uniform. The minute the last line was tied, he would give the order, "Secure from special sea detail; liberty begins at once." We would see him scurrying off the ship about thirty seconds later.

His crew came first in many ways. Most of the time we operated with two other destroyers, and Osborn was the senior officer of the group. As we all tied up and were secured, or sometimes even before, he would call out to the nearest ship's CO, "Oh George, you have shore patrol." That would give our guys one less day of shore patrol.

In August 1942 we entered the Balboa Navy Yard for a major overhaul, going directly into the dry dock. We were to spend the next eight weeks living on a ship out of water. We slept, ate, and worked on the ship, but

Some of the ordnance gang working while in the Navy Yard. From left to right, Fred Bartell, Dick Wenz, me (in front), Jim Allegri, Happy Coburn, and Ed Johnson.

we used navy yard toilet facilities. While in dry dock, we had the stacks and mast cut down to make the *Borie* look more modern and sleek. The mast could be cut down because we were getting radar installed, thus eliminating the crow's-nest lookout watch. More important, we now would be able to "see" the enemy in all kinds of weather, day or night. My job was to oversee the rewiring of the fire-control system and to design a new sound-powered fire-control telephone system, including a switchboard for transferring the circuits. I spent the first week designing the telephone system that, when installed, worked great. The captain put a nice commendation in my service record for that work, and I was never called "Jesus Christ" again.

The rest of the time I kept a check on the yard electricians, cleaned and adjusted all the telescopes, checked all the gun-control systems after they were rewired, and painted all the fire-control stations so that when

Bartell: sober, nice, and working.

Bill Roehrig, at right, hatless and feet nicely balanced. Those two guys were our automatic potato peelers.

we left for sea the fire-control division was in tip-top shape. Most important, I found that I really liked to do meaningful work more than the office work I had done before I was called to active duty.

Many things were done to make the ship battle ready: new camouflage paint, porthole covers, engine room work, and more. But most important, a great many changes were made in our armament and equipment to make us a better hunter and killer of submarines.

Work progressed and time passed so that one morning, when we saw the water start to enter the dock, we knew we would soon be putting out to sea. We were ready.

Our duty remained about the same for the rest of 1942. We did patrol and convoy duty and made occasional sub attacks, but nothing relieved the boredom or got our minds off the possibility of being transferred to a ship heading to the South Pacific.

In October 1942, Lt. Charles ("Hutch") Hutchins, USNR, a Naval Academy graduate, relieved our executive officer.

The United States had been sending convoys down the coast of South America to Brazil and then across to Africa since early in the war. Six ships had been sunk in May and June within twelve hundred miles of the Brazilian coast. With the invasion of Africa planned for November, ship movements via the South Atlantic increased dramatically.

Hitler now made another of his miscalculations: He decided to launch a U-boat blitz against Brazil. He dispatched a group of ten submarines that took up stations close to the Brazilian coast. Between August 14 and 17 they sank five Brazilian merchant ships, including a troopship carrying Brazilian soldiers. Brazil declared war on Germany on August 22. In the short term, that turned out to be very important to us *Borie* sailors. Now that we were allies, we were treated very well by everyone when we went ashore.

November turned into a happy month for us. It had been almost two years to the day since we left our homes for naval service abroad, and now we heard that we were going to Philadelphia, with a good chance we could get a few days of liberty at home. The cruiser *Boise* had been badly shot up and was on its way to the repair yard in Philly. We were ordered to escort it up the East Coast, which we did happily.

When we arrived in Philadelphia, the crew was divided into two liberty sections, and I was fortunate enough to be in the first one. Each section got about three days off, which was just great for most of us because we lived only about three hours away. We hopped on a train and soon were in the Pennsylvania train station in Newark where Stan Hull and I were greeted by Stan's father, who dropped me off at my home.

I had called my folks from the railroad station telling them that I would be there in about ten minutes (that was the first they knew I was home). Of course, the surprise visit created a great deal of excitement and generated an emotional display, but my fondest memory of that night is of my brother. He wasn't home when I called because he worked as a bartender on weekend nights. After the initial welcome at home from family, friends, and neighbors, I went to the bar where my brother Ed worked.

Ed was not only a good bartender, he had a beautiful voice and often sang for the patrons. His most popular request was for "San Francisco," and though I didn't have as good a voice as his, I would sometimes sing with him.

I sneaked into the place and positioned myself at the other end of the crowded bar. A lot of people recognized me because this had been a favorite place for Shrimpy and me. They started to get excited, but I put my finger to my lips to keep them quiet. I also got a fellow to request "San Francisco."

Ed had to be cajoled, of course. It took about six seconds before he started. I quietly moved up to his back, and at a good part for harmony I joined him in singing. After much hugging with Ed and many old friends of the past, we managed to finish the song. I cannot truly describe the warmth I felt, not only for my brother but for all the people who were there that night. If that demonstration of love and affection indicated how the people of the nation felt, our country was behind the war effort 100 percent.

Back in Philly, I had a few nights of liberty. A few of us had an interesting experience. We went to see a navy movie to find out what the war was all about. Remember, that was less than a year after Pearl Harbor. The picture was about a ship exactly like our *Borie,* including a three-inch gun on the stern. They called it an antiaircraft gun but forgot to mention that the aircraft was World War I vintage. In the movie a German dive-bomber attacked, and the gunner on the three-inch gun knocked it down. We all started to hoot and howl and kept it up until the usher informed us we would be ejected if we didn't stop.

Why all the hooting? Because we had target practice with a gun like that, and we couldn't even hit a large, slow-moving balloon!

I was glad we weren't kicked out because the movie was followed by a stage show loaded with scantily clad, beautiful girls. Some of them came out into the audience to grab servicemen, including me, and take them back onto the stage. I never would have gone, but the girl played dirty. She dazzled me with her beautiful, shapely body so I didn't know where I was until I looked out and saw the audience laughing at my skinny legs with my pants rolled up over my knees. I didn't care. My gorgeous partner made everything worthwhile.

We left the dock in a dense fog and started down the Delaware River, none of us very happy. Suddenly a wonderful event took place. We whacked a buoy. We had to go back to the navy yard. It was on a weekend, and I got to go home. I decided it would be a good time to go to church with my mother, which I had never done before. I thought, "I don't need another night on the town." Friday night, when I told her my plans, she said, "Oh, Bobby [only she could call me Bobby], wouldn't you rather go out with your buddies? Besides, I had planned to go to a picnic Sunday." Saturday morning I left for Philadelphia, having learned another of life's lessons.

We received a wonderful Christmas gift for 1942. Although I wasn't aboard, the *Borie* left Cristobal, Panama, on Christmas Eve, headed for New Orleans and some shipyard work. More important than that, it was time for most of us to get our first leave since we left the United States in 1940.

Not knowing about New Orleans, I had asked for and received permission to be home sometime in early January. One of my good friends, Phil Graham, had written to me and asked if I would be best man at his wedding. Captain Osborn had told me that he would give me leave if I could arrange my own transportation. With a little conniving, I arranged to ride a small patrol craft to Miami.

When the trip to New Orleans came up, three other *Borie* men went with me for the first half of crew's leave. Half the ship had the first half of leave time, then the second half took their leave when we returned.

In the middle of my leave I went to Phil's wedding and met my future wife, Doris. Another buddy loaned me his car for the remainder of my leave, and I spent the rest of the time traveling around with Doris. She invited me to her home to take part in a holiday party with family and friends. A lot of people were present, many of whom were speaking German. One man latched on to me and started asking me about torpedoes. I thought, "What the hell have I gotten myself into?" As it turned out, the man's son was in the navy and had just been sent to primary torpedo school, and the man was not a spy. But when Doris and I were married a few months later, all her mail to me was censored.

Leave ended, and it was time to go back to the ship. The four of us met at the Grand Central train station in New York City, prepared for a bang-up trip back to New Orleans. We had booze, glasses, snacks, and even a small tablecloth. The first thing we did upon boarding the train was set up our party table. It was a beautiful thing to behold as we poured our first drink for a toast to the trip back. Our joy only lasted a few minutes. "Hey," someone said. Looking up we saw a huge MP, who fortunately was a good guy. He said, "You better get that shit out of sight or the next guy will lock you up." We had to sneak our drinks from under our seats for the rest of the trip.

We had a layover in Atlanta, and while we were eating lunch we found that Atlanta was a dry city. Now what is the best way to find out where you can go to do what you aren't supposed to do? Ask a cop. I did, and he told us where we would find a speakeasy. We had a great time; we missed our train and arrived in New Orleans a day late.

New Orleans was the best liberty port we had been in since going on active duty. It could have been even better if the admiral commanding the naval district hadn't decided to make the French Quarter off limits. Even so, there was no problem finding something different and exciting to do every time we went ashore.

The ship was in dry dock. We lived on the ship but used the showers, toilets, and best of all, the mess hall on the base. A few weeks earlier, while I was home, my mother explained to me all about rationing. We, the *Borie* crew, had left the United States before rationing started. She told me she didn't mind doing without as long as the "boys" were getting it. I said, "Sure we are." In a pig's eye we were. I don't remember ever having steak. They tried to serve us chicken once, but it turned out to be spoiled. We seldom had fried eggs, and all in all, I don't think our food could have been called gourmet. I didn't blame the navy as much as I blamed the situation. It was hard to get food supplies where we operated, and our food storage facilities were very small.

I did find out who was getting all the good stuff—the guys with shore duty, stationed at navy bases. Eating at the mess hall was an eye-opener. I had steak for the first time, and we had real breakfasts every morning. That was living again! We could even eat without moving our arms in a jogger motion. Something seemed wrong for a couple of meals, until I finally realized I was eating without a foot hanging in my face from the bunk over my head. For a short time I even thought of quitting the outfit for life on shore, but I decided to stay. I really loved the glamorous navy life and seeing the world for free. How else would I get to meet all the beautiful rich blondes?

We didn't know it at the time, but the following message was received late in December 1942. (I found the message in Captain Osborn's war diary recently.) It was to have a profound effect on us, both good and bad.

By ComPaSeaFron despatch 2261440 of December, 1942, this vessel was detached from ComPaSeaFron and ordered to report to CincLant and ComSoLant by despatch.

Reported for duty to CincLant and ComSoLant by despatch 272001 of December, 1942.

That message meant that the *Borie* was reassigned to duty in the South Atlantic, to operate off the coast of South America rather than in the Canal Zone.

USS *Borie (DD215)* underwent yard work in January 1943. Results: replacement of two torpedo mounts with two twenty-millimeter machine gun mounts; addition of a raised tub with two twenty-millimeter machine gun mounts (total twenty-millimeter mounts: six); addition of six depth charge projectors capable of firing a depth charge a good distance away from the ship (the ship also had the original two depth charge racks on the stern); addition of an SA radar. We were to use all of this in one battle.

For the entire month of January we were moored at Todd-Johnson Dry Docks, getting under way on February 6, 1943. With the overhaul completed, we sadly left New Orleans and headed back to Panama, or so we thought. We didn't know what adventures lay in store for us. But we were going to have adventures, believe me.

The yard work in New Orleans in addition to the work already completed in Balboa ensured that *Borie* was better prepared for battle than ever before. Six twenty-millimeter machine guns, surface to air radar, and six depth-charge K guns were installed. Fire-control equipment was overhauled, and new receivers, a rangefinder, and a fire-control gyro were all installed. These additions were needed and used when we once again sailed into harm's way.

You might as well know about our hygienic amenities. We had two showers, which of course isn't bad for about fifty men trying to get ready to go ashore. It wouldn't have been bad except that the circular shower room had a diameter of about two shoulder widths. This wouldn't have been bad either except that there was a hot steam line running down the outer wall, making it awkward to bend over to wash your feet. When we first went aboard the *Borie* we thought that some of the men were so rank-conscious that they were wearing chevrons on their butts, but we soon found out that it only took a slight roll or bump from a fellow showerer to gain another stripe—without pay of course.

The steam pipe came out the wall and ended near the no. 1 crapper. We washed our clothes in buckets. We would fill the bucket with cold water, tell the man, if any, sitting on no. 1 to move his legs, hang the bucket on the steam pipe, and turn on the valve. Instant hot water! Hey, some things were good.

After Pearl Harbor we stood three types of watches while at sea, depending on the considered chance of encountering the enemy: Condition I, all hands at battle stations; Condition II, gun(s) manned, but the men could sleep near the gun(s); Condition III, regular under-way watches.

We finally arrived in Trinidad after a dull trip. On February 13, 1943, the *Borie* was assigned to Escort Unit 23.2.4, which consisted of the USS *Borie*, USS *Goff*, USS *Courage*, USS *Tenacity*, USS *PC-592*, and USS *PC-575*. At 2000, on the thirteenth, our unit left Trinidad in company with convoy TB-5. TB-5 meant convoy no. 5 from Trinidad to Brazil. Osborn was named as escort commander of Escort Unit 23.2.4 while it steamed in company with TB-5.

The trip from Trinidad to Recife was long (about two thousand miles) for the escorts, so for the first time the *Borie* refueled from an oil tanker while under way. I believe that was also the first time for all the other escorts, and much to our surprise all ships refueled without incident. Refueling at sea was to become a frequent occurrence for the *Borie*.

TB-5 proceeded without incident, at least for most of the crew. For the bridge and Captain Osborn it was more interesting. Ships both joined and left the convoy. Some of the convoy didn't cooperate, dumping garbage in daylight, showing lights at night, and similar infractions.

On February 28, Task Unit 23.2.4 was relieved of convoy TB-5 by the Brazilian cruiser *Bahia* and its Brazilian escort vessels, and we proceeded into Recife, Brazil, after fifteen days. Our average speed was about eleven knots, which was considered good. At that speed the trip without zigzagging would have taken about seven days. The distance from Trinidad was about 2,000 miles, but the engine distance on the *Borie* was 4,064 miles!

We thought the trip was without incident as far as enemy action was concerned, but we found out later that subs had been reported in our vicinity and were in a favorable position to attack had they chosen to do so. Convoy escorts and attack submarines had started to jockey for position in the South Atlantic.

Brazil had been an Allied sympathizer since the attack on Pearl Harbor, but out of economic need had allowed Germany and Italy to continue using its airports, even though it had broken diplomatic relations with those countries.

Recife had all the requirements for a good liberty port—nice restaurants, bars, shows, and high-class brothels. After nearly two years of primitive liberties, we were ecstatic with what we found there.

I don't remember exactly how many times we had liberty in Recife, but probably it was about six, and all of them were fantastic. We were paid in Brazilian money, and the exchange rate was twenty to one. During that part of the war we were at sea most of the time, so we had little chance to spend our money, which meant when we went ashore we had a bundle. For my first liberty in Recife I withdrew $100, not realizing that would be $2,000 in Brazilian money (all the other guys did the same sort of thing). I was handed a roll of bills about four inches thick, which I had to carry in my hand because the money wouldn't fit in my pockets or wallet. We started out treating a Brazilian dollar as a nickel, and because of that we made great friends with the local people. Brazil used the same monetary system we did. For example, 100 centavos equaled one cruzeiro (one Brazilian dollar). Suddenly we were all rich.

I spent my first money on a taxi ride from the dock to a restaurant, five cruzeiros. Jimmy and I usually split the bills, but for twenty-five cents I could afford to be a big spender. Hell, I couldn't let the guy go with only twenty-five cents, so I gave him another twenty-five cents. I couldn't understand why he shook my hand so hard for a twenty-five cent tip (I had actually given him ten dollars). About eight of us met at a very nice restaurant, where we all sat at the same table. Again I decided to be generous and ordered steaks for everyone. They were five dollars each or about forty dollars for everyone (two dollars American). When I tipped the waiter, I couldn't give him thirty cents (15 percent of two dollars), so I gave him ten cruzeiros, and I swear he did backflips all the way to the kitchen. That sort of thing happened with all the crew until we learned to think in Brazilian money. Of course, by then all the shopkeepers and everyone else knew we were easy, so they set up two sets of prices, one for Brazilians and one for Americans. Even at the higher prices everything was still a bargain.

Showing off new boots—cheap! Left to right are Jim Aikenhead, Francis McKervey (lost in action), Bill Green (to win the Silver Star), Ed Malaney, and Mousey Moultrop.

Of course, I had to stand shore patrol duty there, and that was always interesting. There wasn't much need for shore patrol in the city proper because the atmosphere was such that a man had to look for trouble if he wanted it. So most of my shore patrol was in the brothels, and that was always interesting. They were nothing like the whorehouses in Panama or Jamaica, which, if you were smart, you avoided like the plague even on shore patrol.

As always, the shore patrol went ashore before the start of regular liberty. And, as always, we headed for the brothel areas. Prostitution was legal, so there was no need to carry out business in dark, sleazy hideaways. Consequently, the houses were nice looking, usually large, and located in clean residential areas. Inside they were well-decorated and usually had a large sitting room where the resident "talent" congregated. In most, but not all of the houses, the women fit the description of call girls, not of streetwalkers, the image that most people get when the word *prostitute* is used. As a matter of fact, there were no streetwalkers in Recife such as were seen in New York, Panama, Casablanca, and most of the ports we visited.

As we approached the brothel area, the first thing we would see were men scurrying out of the houses; we were to discover that those men were Brazilian or British sailors who were welcome only when the Americans were out to sea, unless they were willing to pay the price set for Americans. Most of them couldn't afford that, so out they went.

We would patrol the whole area and inspect all the houses. Then, as in other areas where the houses and girls weren't sleazy, we would pick out one place to sit and talk with the girls until liberty started. In Recife, however, that wasn't easy because Brazil was the one country where nobody spoke English, not even the little kids or taxi drivers. My Spanish wasn't much help either because the residents didn't speak Spanish either. I could pick out written words in newspapers or menus, but as far as speaking or understanding, forget it.

I had been told by a naval dentist in Panama that I would have to have a front tooth pulled because it couldn't be filled. I told him to forget it. While in Recife, I decided to go to a civilian dentist, and I was sure that the dentist, being a college man and living in a predominantly Spanish-speaking continent, would be able to speak and understand Spanish. Wrong! Neither he nor his nurse could understand a word of English or Spanish. What a predicament. I knew that I had a gum-line cavity on an incisor, and I also knew that it could hurt very much when being drilled to prepare it for filling. So now, not being able to tell him how I felt, I became very subtle. I demonstrated that I would knock his block off if he hurt me too much while drilling. This wasn't hard to do because he was a nice little guy, about five feet, four inches tall. He did believe me, however, as he must have started with the smallest drill made and went "zzzt." He then went to successively larger drills giving each one a "zzzt." He never hurt me one little bit, and I still have that tooth fifty years later.

There was a femme fatale operating in the South Atlantic in the port of Bahia. Survivors of torpedoed ships asserted that security was very slightly observed at Bahia where "Torpedo Annie," a beautiful redhead, seduced only men with the rank of master and passed on the information to Germany. She was suspected of supplying information that resulted in the loss of a Liberty ship from BT-6, which was proceeding from Bahia to Trinidad. We assumed escort duty for the convoy at Recife as the convoy moved north.

Convoy duty down and up the coast of South America was dangerous, tedious, and grueling hard work. The trip was about four thousand miles, so we were at sea a long time, for a ship the size of the *Borie*. The duration of the trip varied according to the speed of the slowest ship in the convoy. Some of them were very slow.

Refueling from tankers was necessary on those long trips. That was hard work not only for the crew that handled the hoses, but also for the captain and other personnel on the bridge.

In addition to the expected hardships on long trips in the rough Atlantic, we had another comfort problem. Our refrigerator and fresh food storage capacity was not large enough to supply our needs for much more than a week, so we soon were eating nothing but canned foods and corn bread. It was then that I learned to eat canned pork and beans for breakfast and waxy canned cold cuts for supper. SPAM made its appearance for both the army and navy about then, and it was to be about forty years before most World War II veterans could eat it again.

Another food that was enjoyed by both the army and navy was chipped beef on toast. There has been, and still is, a constant battle about what it was called. My army friends say SOS or shit on a shingle. My navy friends and I say FSOT, which I won't translate. We did have SOS also, but it was ground beef with brown gravy. Anyway, I liked both of them then and still eat both today.

Saturdays were always a super food day, if we didn't want to eat, that is. We had pork and beans for breakfast, bean soup for lunch, and waxed cold cuts for supper. We didn't call them cold cuts; we called them something that had to do with a horse's anatomy.

So, although the newspapers covered the Pacific battles daily, we struggled to get men and material on their way across the Atlantic for the liberation of Europe—hazardous work that went mostly unnoticed. Was it dangerous? In spite of increased convoy protection and the entrance of Brazil (with its navy) into the war, November and December of 1942 were the worst months for sinkings in that part of the Atlantic. Nine merchant ships were sunk in November and twelve in December. Farther east, closer to Africa but for the most part still part of the same convoys, ten more were sunk in November and twenty-five in December.

On March 2, 1943, Task Unit 23.2.4, consisting of the *Borie*, the corvettes *Courage* and *Tenacity*, and *PC-575* and *PC-592*, with the *Borie* in command, left Recife to join convoy BT-6 (Bahia-Trinidad, twenty-nine ships) already under way. The convoy was headed for Trinidad. Convoy speed was only about eight knots, which made us nervous, but adding to that dilemma, a twenty-nine ship, inexperienced convoy is very large for only five escorts.

On the evening of March 3, the SS *Jared Ingersoll* reported a submarine sighting. The convoy commodore executed an emergency turn, signaling the other ships with a light. The whole port side of the convoy turned on their navigational lights, and some of them fired flares. We, the *Borie*, assumed the convoy had been attacked (it hadn't) and conducted an offensive sweep with star shells. There was so much confusion that things couldn't be set straight until daylight. It's a good thing a sub wasn't on our tail or it would have been one hell of a mess. It would not be difficult for a submarine to follow an eight-knot convoy while submerged, then come to the surface and attack during darkness.

At 0020, March 6, our radar picked up a dense formation of ships almost dead ahead. It was Convoy TB-6 (Trinidad-Bahia), which we had expected to pass about twenty miles to port at about dawn. Osborn fired a green star signaling a right turn for the convoy. It was seen by all the escorts but not obeyed by the convoy except for two ships that almost rammed each other. TB-6 passed very close to port, narrowly averting a disaster. With the friends we were playing with, who needed the Germans as enemies?

We didn't need them, but we were to get them soon. I was on watch on the bridge (helm and lookout) when, at 0210, five explosions were heard on the port quarter. CLANG, CLANG, CLANG—"general quarters, general quarters; all hands man your battle stations."

Since I was on watch, I had to wait for my relief before I went to my battle station. Along came Domingo Concha, my relief, excited as all get-out. Mingo, as he was called, was a guy who never got excited, but as he took his place he said over and over, "Ain't this the nuts. Ain't this the nuts." Poor Mingo, one of the best-liked men on the ship, would be lost in action before the year was out.

The convoy commodore ordered an emergency turn to starboard while the *Borie* and side escorts, *PC-592* and *Courage,* conducted offensive sweeps to port. Three ships were severely damaged in the initial attack, *George Meade, Tabitha Brown,* and *Joseph Rodman Drake;* the 3,872-ton British freighter *Kelvinbank* took two direct hits that sent the doomed ship to the bottom amid a series of explosions. What we didn't know was that a single U-boat, *U-510,* had caused that havoc—and more was to come. For the next three hours we swept the waters around the scattered convoy in search of our lethal enemy. Unknown to us, the U-boat was nearby, reloading its tubes and making ready for another attack.

Suddenly, more explosions lit up the night sky as torpedoes struck home again. The *Mark Hanna, James Smith, Thomas Ruffin,* and *James K. Polk* were all hit within a seven-minute period. The *Borie* and the other escorts fired star shells and maneuvered frantically between the ships as the sound operators listened for cavitation noises from the attacker. But with all the noise and chaos around us, it was impossible to detect the enemy and keep any semblance of protective convoy order.

After some time we were able to reassemble what was left of the convoy and proceed to the Gulf of Paria, arriving, exhausted, on March 12. We had had to change convoy course once more when a U.S. Army plane reported a "disappearing target" twelve miles ahead.

The *Courage* and *PC-592* were left behind to pick up survivors. Seven damaged ships were drifting near the attack area, and British and U.S. Navy ships rushed to the scene to take the ships in tow. All seven were located and taken to Trinidad. The *Courage* and *PC-592* picked up 130 survivors.

We continued with BT and TB convoys, getting sound contacts and dropping depth charges, but we were never sure if those attacks were real. No ships were hit, and no submarine debris was sighted.

One convoy, TB-13, did add to my list of life's experiences. My radius of travel before entering the navy was a whopping sixty miles, so I was an expert on buses, trains, trolley cars, hot buildings, and tar roads. But my experience with TB-13 was new. The convoy went farther south, and we passed the mouth of the Amazon River while we were still far out to sea (no land in sight). There was a sharp demarcation line where the ocean met the river. It looked like a crossroads at sea, and it was a very moving experience for me.

On the morning of May 10, 1943, we approached the starboard side of the SS *Frederick R. Kellog* to fuel at sea. Both ships were rolling and yawing considerably as we closed in at about eight knots. At that speed, in those sea conditions, the *Borie* didn't exactly turn like a bicycle. It acted more like a sea turtle. We whacked the other ship good on the starboard quarter and continued scraping from that point aft, for about thirty feet, before the ships separated.

The crew of the SS *Frederick R. Kellog* tried to take credit for that, but we wouldn't let them get away with it. We could prove that our compass error was zero degrees and we knew exactly where we were going.

Our new Ramming Score as of May 10, 1943, was as follows: banana boat in Panama Canal, whale in the Atlantic, airplane in the Pacific, and ship in the South Atlantic convoy. But we weren't finished yet. The "daddy" of them all was still to come.

After another great liberty in Recife, we left port at 0800 on May 26. Rendezvous was effected with BT-14 at 1200. There were ten ships in five columns. Escort Group 42.1 consisted of the *Borie, Courage, PC-592, Saucy,* and *Tenacity*. The convoy speed was set at eight knots.

At 0900 on May 27, the Argentine steamer *Rio Bermejo* was sighted traveling alone at a speed of nine knots. She was not all that far away and on a parallel course. She was warned to keep clear of the convoy and allowed to proceed. Further investigation, however, showed that she had been regarded with suspicion earlier in connection with an attack on a convoy. She had sailed through that convoy, fully lighted, just before the attack.

At 2346, explosions were heard on our sound gear. Red flares and two white flares were seen on the starboard side of the convoy. We immediately went to General Quarters, and with a hard right turn started to echo range (search) for submarines at a speed of seventeen knots. All escorts were ordered to execute search plans. At 2350 we fired two spreads of four-inch, fifty-caliber star shells. No target was located by sight, radar, or sound. An hour later we fired another search spread and saw nothing. All escorts made search sweeps while traveling toward the area of attack. At 0046 we saw a wreck afloat with the *Saucy* and *PC-592* nearby. Osborn ordered them to try to prevent merchant seamen from abandoning ship. That didn't work. The ship was recognized as the SS *Florida*. The *Saucy* and *PC-592* were ordered to return the survivors to the still floating *Florida* and rejoin the convoy after daylight.

At 0500 on May 28, we found that two other vessels, the SS *Cardinal Gibbons* and the SS *John Worthington,* had been hit; however, they continued on with the convoy.

On June 1 at 2245, the steamer SS *Colabee* reported that she had broken down completely. No help could be afforded her so a radio request for assistance was made to the Naval Operating Base in Trinidad. The ship had not been located as of June 6, the day after we arrived in Trinidad.

By now all Americans supported the war effort. They no longer had the "what the hell, it ain't our war" attitude. It was about a year and a half since the attack on Pearl Harbor, two and a half years since the first man had been drafted; by then hardly a family in the country didn't have a loved one serving in some faraway place. Many of those men had been away for one to three years, with no sign of the war ending in the near future. Patriotism and pride swept the nation. Most men worried about not going off to war. Unlike some periods in our history that were to follow, high school and college students left school voluntarily to serve their country. Probably more important, those left at home—mothers, fathers, wives, and sweethearts—gave their all to help the war effort. World War II had become the "good" war, and the nation had bonded as one with great patriotism and an abiding resolution to win. With the war effort at home getting stronger all the time and the military, by now mostly a civilian force, rapidly becoming equal to the best the enemy had, the outcome of the war was inevitable.

The entertainment world also was swept up in the wave of patriotism. Many movie stars enlisted right after Pearl Harbor. Although many did what most American men wanted to do—join the fight—I believe those who stayed behind and performed did as much or more for the morale and well-being of the men away from home. Most ships and bases had movie projectors, and the films were a welcome relief from the day's duties. There were films to make us laugh and films to entertain us, such as musicals, corny war movies, and the usual mysteries and westerns. We watched them all, sometimes many times because to get new films we had to swap with other ships, which wasn't easy.

Just as important to the guys were the pin-up pictures that started to appear after the war started. Pin-up pictures were an entirely different concept then. They were pictures of the most popular and most beautiful movie stars of the day, not at all like the *Playboy* pictures of today. Betty Grable's picture was without a doubt the most popular, and it would be rare to find a ship that didn't have at least one of those well-known pictures in sight. Betty's tush was, I'm sure, patted by more soldiers and sailors than can be imagined, but it was done with affection and respect because the men hoped that, at war's end, they would go home to someone as beautiful.

Most likely what gave the most comfort to both the fighting men, who by now had been away a long time, and their loved ones waiting at home was the music that had been written since the war started. No other era in American history gave us so many great songs and fabulous artists as the years of World War II. There were love songs to rekindle the warmest memories, songs of separated sweethearts and coming home again, songs that kept the love of divided couples strong—all of them with melodies and words that we will never forget and that will last forever. Hearing them today brings back fond memories of the good parts of those heavy days.

I can still picture shipmates in their bunks listening to records or the radio playing those songs. There were many wistful faces as the beautiful words were heard over the quiet rush of the ocean against the sides of the ship as we continued on our mission.

Some of the titles signaled the mood of both the serviceman and those he left behind: "You'll Never Know," "I'll Never Smile Again," "I'll Walk Alone (because I'm lonely)," "When the Lights Go on Again," "Saturday Night (is the loneliest night of the week)," "I'll Be Seeing You," "There Are Such Things (a heart that's true)," and many, many more.

Our crew really appreciated the things Captain Osborn did to make life as nice as possible for us, but those things were visible. He also did things for his men through official channels that we weren't aware of. I found out about some of those efforts fifty years later, when I obtained copies of the *Borie* logbook and his war diary.

One suggestion to the commander of the Fourth Fleet was to have a profound effect on the *Borie*'s crew. I found a long letter from Osborn, dated May 9, 1943, to the commander of the Fourth Fleet. Since the letter is long I'll attempt to show its purpose with a few excerpts.

> At present time numerous escort groups have been established. . . . Some units regularly escort to or from United States ports while others continuously operate between outlying bases. Some of these areas of operation have been in effect for three years . . . (*Borie* group, for example). . . . It is proposed to . . . shift whole groups to other areas. . . .
>
> Improve morale. The vessel in which I am serving has been stationed out of the United States three years and on its present run there is no op-

Capt. Philip R. Osborn (right foreground) and crew receiving tickets to the 1943 Sugar Bowl. Captain Osborn was commanding officer of the *Borie*.

portunity to grant leave. The . . . anticipation of changing home port to the U.S. . . . would have a beneficial effect on the crew and contribute to the general efficiency of the escort units concerned.

Near the end of May 1943, the *Borie, Barry,* and *Goff* were assigned Norfolk, Virginia, as home port. Was it coincidence? I don't think so.

It was not without some regret, however, because Capt. Phil Osborn was relieved as commanding officer. His was going to be a hard act to follow, but his replacement, Lt. Charles (Chuck) Hutchins, was to do a good job. When he took command of the *Borie* at age thirty-nine, he became the youngest commanding officer of a destroyer in the U.S. Navy.

We, at least the crew, didn't know what our new assignment was to be, but our duties were about to change dramatically.

⚓

PART THREE

On Patrol in the Atlantic
with TG 21.14

After being detached from the South Atlantic Forces we wasted no time getting into what was to be *Borie*'s last six months afloat. The crew was about to experience some very exciting and dangerous events, and I, the city kid, was about to be exposed to more experiences that would change my attitude about what's really important in life.

Our escort group consisted of the USS *Borie (DD215),* commanding officer, Lt. Charles Hutchins; USS *Goff (DD247),* commanding officer, Lt. Cdr. H.I. Smith; and USS *Barry (DD248),* commanding officer, Lt. Cdr. H.D. Hill.

We found ourselves heading east, instead of south, in the latter part of May. We headed east and east and then we headed east. Had I not read about Christopher Columbus in high school I would have worried about falling off the edge. But not to worry, we had a landfall, and we could smell it! Not good either.

New commanding officer of the *Borie,* Lt. Charles Hutchins (right), the youngest destroyer commanding officer in the United States Navy at that time.

We entered the harbor of Casablanca, French Morocco, and it was a mess. Sunken and damaged French ships were everywhere, and a thick layer of fuel oil covered the entire harbor; it had a stench you wouldn't believe. All this damage was done by United States forces about six months earlier when the Allies made their first major amphibious invasion of the war on the beaches of Morocco. The Allies pleaded with the Vichy French forces to join them and help in the struggle to free Europe from German aggression. Because of false pride, or whatever, the French forces fired on the Allied invasion forces. It was a bad decision.

We tied up at a dock for the usual fuel, food, and other supplies, but the operation soon turned into mass confusion. A truck arrived with bread for us. It turned out to be a dump truck that backed up to the dock and dumped a pile of unwrapped, round loaves of black rye bread on the dirty dock deck. From then on everything went downhill.

Next, a guy dressed in (more or less) white robes appeared. He had a beard, wore a long, flowing robe, and had a turban on his head. He was a real, live Arab.

He was soon joined by more similarly dressed men, all with beards and all carrying fistfuls of American dollars. They lined up along the side of the ship, and it became apparent that they wanted to buy stuff; in fact, it seemed they would buy anything. One Arab came close to a torpedo man who was cleaning torpedo warheads with rags he pulled from a bale of assorted clean rags. The Arab pointed at the rags, and the torpedo man, thinking he was asking for a piece of rag, pulled out a rag about the size of a face towel and threw it to him. The guy ran up for the rag and handed the torpedo man a dollar. You know what happened after that, but the open bartering for government property was soon halted. However, that didn't keep the ingenious sailor from making a buck.

Although the Arabs appeared to be poor, they seemed to have an endless supply of American money. Two of their favorite items were mattress covers, long pillow covers that we used in place of sheets, and fountain pens. We paid ninety cents for the covers and sold them to the Arabs for ten dollars. They bought all they could get. The story was that clean white sheets were required to bury their dead. I don't remember the going price for fountain pens, but Jim Aikenhead told me he made enough money to set himself up with a small trucking company. As you will see later, it was highly unlikely that he was able to get all that money home.

The movie *Casablanca* had been released in 1942, so we couldn't wait to visit "Rick's Place." If you saw that fine picture, you can well imagine why we anticipated visiting the city.

As we arrived and started to mingle with the people, the first thing I realized (after wondering where *Casablanca* was filmed) was that we were not in a pro-American area. We were constantly surrounded by men and boys trying to sell us everything imaginable, but there were no smiling faces, and sometimes the atmosphere was downright scary.

There were Arabs with camels everywhere. The area fascinated me, although I did become disenchanted with camels; they could spit better than most American baseball pitchers. Overall, observing a style of living from out of the past was an interesting experience, but Casablanca certainly wasn't much of a liberty port. At that moment I would have preferred Norfolk, Virginia. No sailor of the World War II era would ever believe that statement.

The crew had been briefed about what to expect while on liberty, including the hostility of the Arabs, and also what to avoid. One of the things that was stressed most was not to drink the water—under any circumstances. Jimmy Allegri, Eddie Johnson, and I had lunch together. The only menu item that made sense was fried eggs. How could they screw up fried eggs with water? So, under orders, we ordered wine with our eggs. Noticing something about the taste after a couple swigs, I decided to continue drinking the wine with eggs hoping to discover what this delicate addition was. I finished two more bottles but never did identify what it was; I didn't care either. Several of the men weren't careful enough about the water and regretted it, especially if they lived in the forward crew's compartment. It was about a fifty-yard dash to the head. Not everybody who started the race made a clean finish. The navy called the problem dysentery; my mother called it "the green apple two-step"; but whatever you called it, it made Montezuma's revenge pale by comparison.

I started home by myself, avoiding camels, and walked casually, taking in all the strange and different sights. A small boy approached me and put out his hand as if to shake hands. I thought he was a beggar and was going to hit me up for some money, but I put my hand out in return anyway. Not knowing why I did it, I put my thumb down and pressed it against a gold ring that I was wearing. This kid turned out not to be a beggar but a bugger. He tried to strip the ring from my finger! He would have gotten it too if my thumb hadn't been there. I had enough time to crack him across the head with the back of my hand. I didn't hit him very hard, but he went down screaming something in Arabic. I had forgotten everything I knew about the language, so I don't know what he hollered, but everyone nearby did. Suddenly about ten or so Arabs came running at me, screaming. I took off with them running after me, and probably the only reason they didn't catch me and chop my hand off was because they were wearing long flowing robes.

Quite a few of the men had trouble with the Arabs, partly because they appeared to hate us and partly because we didn't understand their customs. The most serious incident involved one of our sailors and a prostitute. When he was safely back on the ship, he told his story. He wasn't clear about how he knew which woman to proposition because they all looked and smelled the same. They were not seductive looking at all with their veils and bulky dark robes. Why he would want to beats the heck out of me, but somehow he persuaded a woman into a deal. He found himself with her in a vacant room, no furniture at all, and everything going as planned—almost. He had been able to talk her into having sex, probably because she was very poor, but she refused to remove her veil. The dummy reached up and tore it off her face. He had just committed an unforgivable sin in their religion. Her screaming brought a horde of Arab men. Luckily he was still dressed. He managed to escape from a howling posse in flying robes, although I'm sure his mob was larger and angrier than mine. We heard that Arabs have a very unusual punishment for a crime like that—one that was guaranteed to reduce the desires that got a man into those situations.

While writing this story I started thinking about that man. He was a Damon Runyan character from the New York area, and everybody liked him. He could make us laugh just by talking, but some of his stories fractured us. Sometimes the stories were funny because we couldn't believe he was telling them to us. I never knew anyone before who would reveal such personal details, but this fellow just came across as funny, and no one passed judgment on him.

He had a growl, instead of a voice, and when he addressed anyone he always prefaced the name with "Hey." He was a Catholic, but he almost never went to church. He and I were standing next to each other while the ship was pulling up to a dock early on a Sunday morning. He turned to me and said, "Hey Maahher, I think I'm going to confession today; I haven't been for a long time." I said, "Why?" He answered, "Insurance." Now this guy did zillions of things that required confession according to his church, so I asked, "Jesus, what will you tell the priest?" "Aaahh, I'll tell him that I lied ten times, had sex ten times [he wasn't married], and took the Lord's name in vain ten times." He needed a special confession just for that last statement because his sentences always had at least five expletives.

He was about the same age as most of us, nineteen to twenty-two, but his lifestyle had been very different. He was a city kid, but he hadn't had a regular job. He was part of a shady group, and he made his living as a bookie and by collecting money from pinball machines that his mini-mob had placed in stores close to his home. Joining the navy changed his life for the better; when he was discharged he married and became an outstanding citizen.

There is a reason for recounting these stories, in addition to general interest in the life of a sailor. On one of our trips we received our mail while in Casablanca. I got a letter from my wife, Doris, that was very disturbing. She worked in the stockroom of a factory, and a fellow employee started to make sexual advances toward her and tried to corner her in the stockroom. He knew that I was at sea and not likely to get home for a while. Typical of men who think they are God's gift to women, he continually pointed out how lucky she was to have someone like him around to take my place. The worst thing was that he frightened her by literally trying to trap her against a wall (she worked alone), and she was too embarrassed to tell anyone. I was sitting next to the Runyan character while reading the letter, and I said, "Jesus Christ, what does she expect me to do?" He asked me what the problem was, and when I told him he asked, "Want me to take care of that?" "Can you do that?" "Easy, what do you want me to do? Have him beat up and give him a message? Have him killed?" I shouted, "Hell no, I don't want him killed. I just want him to let her alone." "No problem." And the problem ended.

Next day I decided I would stay in the docking area. I still hadn't gotten over the urine smell that pervaded a large part of the town. The sanitary sewer system was a shallow stone gutter that passed directly through the town square. A couple of us decided to walk around the docks and see the ships that were tied up in the harbor, the French battleship *Jean Bart,* permanently out of action, and a French destroyer sunk at a dock. It made us sad to see that destruction, realizing that the crews had no say in the decision to oppose the forces that were trying to liberate their country from the enemy that occupied it.

We did get to go aboard a Free French destroyer that was fighting on the side of the Allies and were treated royally. We offered to give three French sailors a tour of our ship, but when we asked for permission to do so, the OD refused. Feeling very sheepish, we walked back to their ship and spent more time with them.

Before we left the exotic, smelly city of Casablanca I had a day of shore patrol duty. It turned out to be a fun, if scary, day. I was told that, for personal safety, I would be doing the patrol with the local military police. A U.S. Army jeep came alongside the ship, driven by a Free French army major. He looked sharp, in crisp khaki shorts, khaki shirt, and armed with a holstered automatic pistol (I also carried an automatic pistol). In the back of the jeep, sitting on the top of the back seat with his feet on the seat, was a Senegal soldier (Senegal at that time was a part of French West Africa). Magnificent in a black tunic and white pants, and wearing a red fez with a black tassel hanging from the crown, he looked seven feet tall. The rifle he carried on his knees seemed even longer.

I sat alongside the major, and since my knowledge of French ended after I said "oui," I was happy to find that he spoke excellent English with a charming French accent. But the major was a maniac once he started the engine and we took off. There were no posted speed limits, and he adjusted his speed according to the width of the roads, going only twenty miles per hour faster than was safe. I never had been in a Jeep before, but I had read about their propensity for turning over because of their short turning radius. The major had never read about that, so of course, there was no problem. He made ninety-degree turns, at high speed, into cobblestone roads that were only about four or five feet wider than the Jeep. Once I realized that that was the way it would be, I sat back and started to enjoy the tour. The major was an exciting guy, always laughing and maintaining a running commentary about the things we saw, many of which were unbelievable.

One section of the city was off limits to Allied personnel (by orders of the Allied command, not the Arabs). It was guarded by Legionnaires, and rumor had it that there was a very good chance any Allied serviceman who entered that section through the arched opening would be dead by morning. Upon walking up to the wall that separated that section from the rest of the area, I decided there was no way I would enter that place, even if it hadn't been declared off limits. After a tour of the surrounding area, during which the major showed me many interesting places, we headed for the forbidden section, which he called "La Ville de Mille Femmes." That means "the Town of the Thousand Women."

As we approached the entrance, I asked the reason for the Senegal soldier and rifle. The major pointed to the tops of the buildings (about thirty feet high) and told me that the soldier's job was to keep his eyes above us, with his rifle loaded and ready to shoot to kill if an Arab appeared. Apparently a favorite sport was dropping boulders onto the heads of strangers, especially Allied sympathizers. The place with its dirty shops, cripples, and beggars seemed unbelievable. Americans worry if meat is on the counter of an air-conditioned room for more than a couple of hours.

We passed a meat "store" with cutouts in the stone wall for a door and window. Spoiled-looking meat hung from overhead in disarray, amid a cloud of flies. The major showed me a building where one could pay for girls to dance and play other games. He also said that none of the rooms in that building had roofs so all of the intellectual entertainment could be enjoyed under the stars. We toured the area without any dangerous incident, and I left the Jeep after arriving alongside the *Borie,* grateful for finding a new friend who had provided me with another experience that couldn't be duplicated. I never saw the major again, unfortunately.

On June 9 our escort group, *Borie, Barry,* and *Goff,* left Casablanca harbor for a new duty with new adventures. We didn't know what the new duty would be, but soon found out it was more like the navy than convoy duty.

Upon clearing the harbor we rendezvoused with an aircraft carrier! This was a "hot damn" situation, as we found that we were now part of one of the recently formed carrier escort groups. Our group was designated Task Group (TG) 21.14. TG 21.14 consisted of the escort carrier USS *Card (CVE 11),* commanded by Capt. Arnold J. "Buster" Isbell, and our group of destroyers: USS *Borie (DD215),* USS *Barry (DD148),* and USS *Goff (DD147).* The first such groups actually were part of the convoys and provided an air umbrella for the entire trip. Although the system was effective in deterring submarine attacks, it did little to solve the big problem of destroying the German U-boat fleet. Captain Isbell's plan for using TG 21.14 on the westbound convoy from Casablanca was both to protect the convoy and to start the downfall of the U-boat campaign. Our destroyer group, now relieved from convoy duty, was going to be part of that, and we were thrilled with our new assignment.

Captain Isbell decided that it wasn't necessary to keep a continuous umbrella over the convoy. Instead, the group would operate independently against any reported concentration of U-boats and get back to the convoy if needed. The plan was so successful that the escort carrier groups soon evolved into independent hunter-killer groups.

TG 21.14 was escorting Convoy *GUS-8* back to the United States, but we were not tied close to the convoy; we could roam about its course. Perhaps that would keep the subs down, or even better, maybe we could locate and sink them before they could attack. The convoy proceeded without incident, arriving safely at Hampton Roads, Virginia, on July 5. It had been an interesting trip for us, however, as we learned how to operate with a carrier.

Of course, the primary job of the destroyers was to protect the carrier from submarine attacks at all costs, but we served other important functions as well. During launching and recovery of aircraft, all escorts were ready to rescue the crew in the event a plane went into the ocean, either by accident or because of battle damage. The aircraft used while we were a part of TG 21.14, Avengers and Wildcats, sank very quickly, in some cases in as little as thirty seconds.

Our three destroyers rotated another very important and very trying (on the nerves) duty: plane guard. As planes were launched and recovered, one of the destroyers would have plane guard duty. It would take a position directly astern the *Card,* ready to rescue a crew if a takeoff or recovery failed, both of which happened. The most difficult and nerve-racking part of that duty, especially for the bridge and engine room crews, was that the ship had to maintain a precise position: a given distance to the rear and along the centerline of the flight deck. When the plane guard maintained that exact position, the runway was artificially lengthened, allowing the pilot to make his approach using the plane guard as part of the "runway." (You might wonder why that was necessary because the flight deck of the *Card* was almost five hundred feet long.) Think about a thousand feet for the larger fast attack carriers, flying about the same type of aircraft. Then compare even one thousand feet with ten thousand feet for most of today's commercial airports.

The officer of the deck had to make many changes in speed to keep the proper distance, driving the engine room nuts; he also made many heading changes, driving the helmsman (including me) nuts. But we did it, and it was the type of activity that made the job fun.

Now we received another surprise. Instead of joining the *Card* in Norfolk, we proceeded to the Brooklyn Navy Yard for equipment changes to make our ship a more efficient member of TG 21.14, which on our next trip would be described as a very real hunter-killer group.

Because about 75 percent of the crew lived close enough to get home on every liberty, you can imagine the excitement as we made the short trip to Brooklyn. Liberty in New York City was a dream of all sailors: big league ball games, stage door canteen, dances and parties, Broadway shows, bars of all kinds. You name it, and it could be found in the city. Best of all, most of the activities were free to servicemen. So even those who didn't have family in the area were dancing on air with anticipation, maybe even more excited. You must always keep in mind that most of the men were young, in their early twenties, and a city like New York could present activities to enjoy that wouldn't be possible under the watchful eyes of mom. Even I probably did a thing or two that would have upset my mom, and if I did, it sure as hell was fun.

Work started as soon as the ship was secured. I must say that the ship-yard workers I talked to were patriotic and completely dedicated to their work. They did their best to get us out, not only quickly but also outfitted to the best of their ability. They felt that their status as defense workers was just as important to their country as the fighting men were; they were right as far as I was concerned.

All of us wanted to stay in New York forever, or even maybe a day or two more, but on July 27, destroyers of TG 21.14 rendezvoused with the *Card,* and we started on our first real hunter-killer mission, while protecting a convoy. Our motto was "get 'em before they get us." The *Card* had the same air squadron (VC-1) aboard that operated on the last trip (Casablanca to Norfolk). It consisted of six F4F-4s (fighters) and eleven TBF-1s (torpedo bombers) commanded by Lt. Comdr. Carl E. Jones.

TG 21.14 pulled into Bermuda, where the *Card* took on fuel, but no liberty was allowed. We left Bermuda early on the morning of July 30, heading east again. Having done that once before, I was no longer afraid of falling off the end of the earth, at least not very much. We caught sight of our convoy early on August 1, and it was a big one. We joined the convoy, *UGS-13,* and as early as that afternoon we had a sign that the mission might turn out to be very interesting. The *Barry* reported a solid sound contact and took off, bow rising with the increasing speed, to the sound of "whoop, whoop, whoop," to make a depth charge run. The *Barry* made about three passes, dropping depth bombs on each one. On the *Borie* we first heard a thundering BOOM, then felt a solid blow to our hull even at quite a distance. As each bomb exploded, a column of water rose from the ocean's surface looking much like Yellowstone Park's Old Faithful geyser. The *Barry* resumed station without any real evidence of a successful attack; however, it was exciting for the escort crews because we knew that U-boats rarely hunted alone.

The *Borie, Barry,* and *Goff* refueled from a tanker in the convoy that same afternoon. We should have known something was in the wind because at 0200, August 2, we (TG 21.14) slipped away from the convoy to search for U-boats, per Captain Isbell's plan. I would have loved to see the look on the faces of all those people who discovered at the dawn's first

USS *Borie* in New York Navy Yard, where a shield forward of gun no. 1 was installed to reduce the force of waves breaking over the bow. Sitting on starboard, forward, is Ralph Long, CCSTD. He had only a few months more to live.

When new Vanish Clear Drop-Ins is in your tank...<u>clear</u>, invisible cleaning power is in your bowl.

New!

VANISH Clear DROP-INS

WORKS LIKE A **BLEACH** CONCENTRATE

DANGER: SOLID MATERIAL CAN BURN EYES AND SKIN. HARMFUL IF SWALLOWED. Read Package Back Carefully.

Introducing Vanish® Clear Drop-Ins.™ A new kind of bowl cleaner with clear, invisible power. With Vanish Clear Drop-Ins, every flush releases tough detergents. It works like a bleach concentrate, but without that bleach smell. So flush after flush, week after week, it helps your bowl stay clean, fresh and crystal clear.

Vanish. When clean really counts.

Try it now.

© 1992 The Drackett Company

The Ultimate Tribute to Our Nation's Freedom

Plate shown smaller than actual size of 8" in diameter.

American Eagle
by Ronald Van Ruyckevelt

A Limited Edition Collector Plate.
Hand-Numbered and Bordered in 24 Karat Gold.

The USS *Card (CVE 11)* and aircraft. It is the destroyer's duty to protect the *Card* even if it means the loss of the destroyer and crew. Seven Avenger bombers and six Wildcat fighters are on the flight deck.

light that their protectors had disappeared. They didn't know that our disappearance offered them the very best protection possible. We were going to start "getting 'em" before they got us. Captain Isbell's plan was the direct approach, nothing fancy, just rush TG 21.14 directly to the center of any reported concentrations of U-boats.

You ask, "Who reported those concentrations, and how did they know?" It's a good question. The reports were the result of the triangulation of bearings taken with high-frequency radio direction finders, nicknamed "Huff-Duff." Huff-Duff was carried aboard ship and also positioned on shore on both sides of the Atlantic. The U-boats would surface, day and night, and converse with each other and U-boat headquarters in Germany. I'm sure the German U-boat high command was aware of those detection stations but didn't feel threatened by them. They used a very complicated machine, called the Enigma, to code and decode their messages and were convinced their cipher system was unbreakable. What they didn't know was that the British had captured a U-boat, *U-110,* in May 1941, with an Enigma machine, complete with cipher system. That stroke of luck, along with the Germans' false sense of security, surely helped turn the tide in the Battle of the Atlantic. Reports of the locations of U-boat concentrations were amazingly accurate when their positions were within range of land-based aircraft. Of course Huff-Duff wasn't much help when a wolf pack was located, mid-ocean, in the path of a large convoy. It wasn't much help, that is, until the hunter-killer groups went on the offensive, as we were about to do.

Huff-Duff scored again! The very next morning, August 3, Lieutenant (jg) Cormier's Avenger bomber, escorted by Ensign Paulson's Wildcat fighter, caught Kapitänleutnant Friedrich Markworth's *U-66* (type IXC U-boat) cruising on the surface about five hundred miles west-southwest of Flores (Azores). Paulson, streaking in low, caught it by surprise, strafed the entire length of the boat, and fatally wounded the officer of the deck. The men on deck gave the diving alarm, but Markworth canceled the order, determined to follow the current fight-back orders from the U-boat high command. Cormier, just behind Paulson, let go his bombs, but they didn't release.

Paulson, now under attack himself, strafed again, and Cormier came in for another bombing run. That time he not only pressed the electrical release but also pulled his emergency release, dropping two depth bombs and a Fido. Fido was a target-seeking torpedo normally used against submerged submarines. Cormier could see a shock wave form to the right and forward of the conning tower and then spread under *U-66* to the port side. A huge column of water, more than a hundred feet high, completely blocked the sub from view. Although Markworth was seriously wounded, *U-66* was able to escape with the second officer in command. When the fighter pilot, Paulson, landed, he was as white as a ghost and had to be taken to sick bay. That was not unusual for a man when, for the first time, he realized he had possibly killed people and also, with sudden reality, that he too could be killed.

That night there was a great deal of radio traffic between *U-66,* the U-boat command, and *U-117* (type XB U-boat), a minelaying submarine. *U-66* was ordered to rendezvous with *U-117* for assistance. Thanks to the Enigma capture and Huff-Duff, we were on to their plans. Consequently, the *Card* and her escorts were ordered to the general area of the rendezvous.

They searched and searched. Then, on August 7, Lt. (jg) Asbury H. Sallenger, flying his TBF bomber, saw something about twelve miles off to his right. Sneaking in for a closer look, he found that something was, indeed, two subs: *U-66* and the minelayer *U-117.* It never ceased to amaze us that we could find submarines operating together on the surface, in broad daylight. Sallenger first radioed the *Card* for support and then, circling so that he could attack from out of the sun, started his bombing run.

The two U-boats continued running on the surface unaware of the impending attack until Sallenger was about four hundred yards away. Both boats suddenly opened up with heavy antiaircraft fire; the fire was intense, but it was inaccurate. Sallenger reported later, "Their firing was rotten. It was all around me, but no hits."

Now U-66 started to submerge so Sallenger, braving the fire of U-117 as he passed alongside it at only two hundred feet and 130 knots, immediately attacked U-66, dropping a Fido. That time Fido's "nose" didn't work and it didn't find the "hydrant" it was looking for. U-66 had escaped again.

With the heavily armed U-117 seemingly trapped on the surface, Sallenger wisely decided to wait for reinforcements. Two Avengers (bombers) and two Wildcats (fighters) charged into the area, and the Wildcats immediately began strafing attacks. Lt. (jg) Ernest E. Jackson and Lt. (jg) Norman D. Hodson, the fighter pilots, wreaked havoc on the U-boat. Even though U-117 had recently acquired the latest antiaircraft weapons, their firing had little effect on the attacking Card aircraft.

Diving on the sub, Lt. (jg) Charles Stapler's bombs hit near the bow on the port side, causing huge columns of water almost to swamp the boat. Soon after, Lt. (jg) Junior C. Forney's Avenger dropped bombs that hit close to the starboard quarter (stern). Determined not to let U-117 get away, the fighters once again streaked in, making several more strafing runs.

U-117 obviously was in trouble. Slowing down and turning, it started to submerge. However, before the Avengers could attack again, the boat slowly surfaced and seemed to flounder about. Then the bow came up, and the conning tower disappeared under the water. Quickly the bow submerged again. It was unclear whether the sub was sinking or attempting to dive and escape. It was a moot point, however, because both Stapler and Forney dropped Fidos, Stapler's on the starboard side and Forney's on the port side. Much churning at the surface, combined with a large area of bubbles, left no doubt that U-117 was out of the war forever.

The next morning, August 8, Sallenger was out on patrol in his Avenger again, escorted by Ens. John F. Sprague in a Wildcat. It wasn't a great day for flying because there were many low-hanging clouds and occasional rain squalls. Coming out of the clouds, Sallenger looked down and could have spit on two subs directly below him. The sudden discovery didn't give him enough time to radio the Card; he attacked at once. Sprague streaked in, raking the nearest submarine with accurate machine-gun fire.

Both boats returned the fire, filling the air with lead. Sallenger's Avenger received the brunt of it as he bore in for his bomb run. His plane

The Grumman TBF Avenger, torpedo bomber.

The Grumman F4F Wildcat fighter.

was hit several times, a fire started in his bomb bay, and his radio and electrical systems were knocked out. Because of the damage, he couldn't release his bombs on that pass. But the accurate gunfire didn't stop him. He circled back for another attack while Sprague continued his strafing runs.

Diving in for the second attack, Sallenger's Avenger was again hit heavily, and a fire started in the left wing. His gunner, AMM3c James H. O'Hagen, said later, "Our electrical system was shot up, and I couldn't work the turret or get in touch with Mr. Sallenger. I called to our radio-man, John D. Downes, to ask him to help me turn my turret around as it was stuck. I looked down in the tunnel and he was lying on his face. The radio equipment was on the deck by his feet, the camera by his side smashed."

Still, Sallenger continued on his bombing run, dropping two depth bombs manually. They both exploded near *U-664* (type VIIC U-boat). Flying on, he dumped his Fido and prepared to ditch his fatally damaged plane. He knew that ditching his Avenger would not be easy. In fact, it turned out to be damned rough when the aircraft hit the water with flaps up and the bomb bay doors open. Sallenger and O'Hagan emerged quickly and started to inflate their raft, but Sallenger noticed that Downes was not in sight. The brave pilot swam under the TBF to see if he could get his radioman out through the tunnel door, but the Avenger started to settle quickly and disappeared in less than thirty seconds, taking Downes with it.

Pilot Sprague and his Wildcat fighter fared much worse. While continuing his strafing runs, still under machine-gun fire, Sprague's plane was shot down by *U-262*, and he was killed.

When the planes failed to return, Captain Isbell sent the *Barry* and six aircraft to Sallenger's search sector. One of the planes located their raft and guided the *Barry* to the downed airmen. Six hours after climbing into the raft, they were aboard the *Barry*. Sallenger called the *Card* on the TBS (talk between ships) radio, a short-range radio for ship/plane to ship talk, and all hands heard him describe the battle.

The *Borie* had not been idle either. While screening the *Card*'s port bow, we got a sound contact off our port side. We made our depth charge runs, dropping sixteen bombs. We knew by now that Huff-Duff hadn't lied; the area was crawling with subs, so we resumed our station. Our carrier and its hunter-killer group were much more valuable than one sub that might or might not be there.

U-262, heavily damaged by Sallenger and Sprague, was forced to return to home base after transferring its extra fuel and supplies to *U-664* and *U-760*. *U-664* was supposed to head for the American coast after taking the supplies from *U-262*, but it stayed in the general area.

As dusk was falling, TG 21.14 also remained in the area, still searching. The watch officer of *U-664*, which wasn't supposed to be there, saw a

Ens. John Franklyn Sprague, killed by machine gun fire from *U-262* while making multiple strafing runs against *U-664* and *U-262*. (Official U.S. Navy photograph)

large "tanker" and called the boat's commander, Kapitänleutnant Adolf Graef, to the bridge. Graef's first name suited him perfectly. His men disliked him intensely and called him a martinet. He had none of the skills needed to be a U-boat commander. He lacked compassion and was completely insensitive to the problems of his crew. He was lazy, mean to his men, and worst of all, he was a lousy shot. The wonder was how he warranted command of a submarine. The U-boat force was entirely voluntary and known to be nonpolitical.

Graef set up the action-torpedo problem and fired three torpedoes at the "tanker." Swoosh, swoosh, swoosh. Nothing. All shots missed, and the target, the Card, plus the escorts, sailed on. We never knew it, but with a more skillful skipper, U-664 could have been cause for an unpleasant evening for some members of TG 21.14.

Probably at about the same time Graef wasted three torpedoes, Captain Isbell was with Lieutenant Commander Jones, the commander of VC-1. They were trying to devise a defense against the U-boats' new "fight-back" tactics. The idea seemed to be working. Probably surprise made the German plan look good at first, but it would be abandoned in the not too distant future.

The air attack teams were now changed from one Avenger and one Wildcat to two Avengers and one Wildcat. One Avenger was to carry two instantaneously fused five-hundred-pound bombs (surface attack), while the other would carry depth bombs and good old dog, Fido. The next afternoon, August 9, was to determine whether the plan worked. Luckily, we ended up with the right man in the right place at the right time: Adolf Graef in U-664.

Suddenly emerging from a cloud, the crews of the three-plane team spotted U-664 only a couple of miles away, cruising on the surface with decks awash. Lt. (jg) Gerald G. Hogan, flying an Avenger with the five-hundred-pound bombs, climbed a thousand feet to set up for his bombing attack. At that altitude he radioed the Card of the sighting and nosed down into his high-speed dive at an angle of fifty degrees.

Lt. Norman D. Hodson's Wildcat was a little closer, so he streaked in and started strafing only seconds before Hogan dropped one of his five-hundred-pound bombs. U-664 had started to submerge, so Hogan could see only the stern and the conning tower, which bore the blue sawfish emblem of the Ninth Submarine Flotilla.

Lieutenant Hogan was in his dive, with the wind howling, as he dropped his bomb from about 750 feet. The bomb hit about twenty feet off the port bow. Lt. (jg) Junior C. Forney, flying the Avenger with depth charges and Fido, charged in from the starboard quarter only ten seconds behind Hogan, and he dropped his two depth charges set to explode at a depth of twenty-five feet. When he dropped the bombs, he was flying at an altitude of a hundred feet, a gutsy pilot indeed. At that altitude and speed, where a slight downdraft could cause him to crash into the sub or the sea, he turned his head and saw his bombs explode beneath U-664 and stop its dive.

Now the result of Graef's arrogance, meanness, and poor qualifications as a submarine commander reared its ugly head. (This information was revealed during interrogation of U-664 survivors.) U-664 came to the surface much like an apple in the child's game "bobbing for apples." All hell broke loose as many of the men forgot discipline and emergency training. In fact, they panicked. The situation got even worse when the engineering officer, stationed in the conning tower, shouted, "Permission to abandon ship?" Hearing the words "abandon ship," fourteen of the crew quickly climbed through the conning tower hatch onto the bridge—a fatal move. Hodson on his way back cleared the bridge with his machine guns, killing some of the men and at the same time starting a fire aft of the conning tower.

It took Graef a little while to get his head together, and then he decided to submerge again. That was probably another bad move, as Hogan helped him along with another five-hundred-pound bomb. The original attack team could see by now that U-664 was in trouble, and Forney decided not to use his Fido. Two Avengers bore in for an attack. A five-hundred-pound bomb was dropped just forward of the bow and another one just aft of the stern. Not to be outdone, a Wildcat strafed the boat from bow to stern again, followed by another Avenger that didn't do as well, dropping its bombs and missing by two hundred feet. By then, even a commander like Graef understood that he wasn't going to get even a draw in the game. I guess a sinking boat gives one a pretty powerful message.

Graef's gang scrambled out of the boat, jumped right into the sea, and swam away as fast as they could. They swam toward eleven rafts that were strung out aft of the doomed U-boat. No sooner had the men left the boat than the bow pointed straight up, and the boat went down, stern first, at 1420.

The Borie was ordered to pick up survivors from U-664. That turned out to be a major operation because many of the men had been wounded by the strafing, some of them badly. As usual, the sea was rough, and the

First bombed by a 500-pound bomb from Lieutenant (jg) Hogan, then two depth charges from Lieutenant (jg) Forney, *U-664* pops to the surface, and its crew prepares to abandon ship. The sawfish on the side of the conning tower is the logo of the Ninth Submarine Flotilla. (Official U.S. Navy photograph)

Borie was doing its normal rolling, bobbing, and weaving. It was obvious that transferring the Germans, especially the wounded, from the rafts to our decks was going to require master seamanship. The slower the forward movement, the worse the ship rolled, and since we would be stopped, that was about as slow as we could go.

As the *Borie* approached the men, their faces bore expressions of fear and apprehension. With Hutchins's careful maneuvering, however, it soon became apparent to them that a bona fide rescue mission was being attempted.

Ladder rungs were welded on both sides of our ship, extending from the deck to the waterline. Earlier, Bill Roehrig had slid overboard while sleeping and used one of those ladders to climb to safety. We also used them for swimming parties while at anchor. Two of the best sailors on the

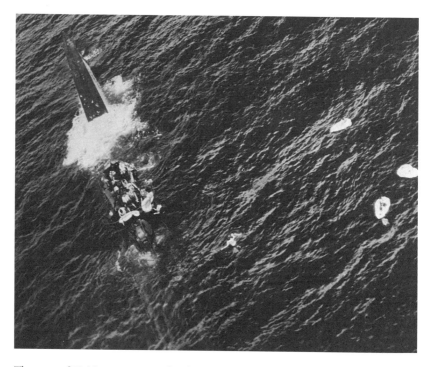

The crew of *U-664* continues to abandon ship as the stern goes deeper. Individual life rafts can be seen at right of the photo, and the crewman at center has not yet inflated his raft. (Official U.S. Navy photograph)

ship, who were also two of the strongest, volunteered to go into the water to expedite the rescue. Chief Boatswain's Mate Walter Kurz and Chief Gunner's Mate Dick Wenz climbed down the port sea ladder, prepared to help the prisoners. At first glance that might seem easy, but it wasn't. Physically they were in a dangerous spot; as the ship rolled, the bottom rung sometimes moved up suddenly and sometimes dropped under the water, carrying Kurz and Wenz in both directions. No one knew how the Germans were going to react to that treatment, especially the wounded. The task was a dangerous responsibility and a brave act for those men. They did their work superbly, helping the Germans up the side, some with blood dripping from their wounds.

For the first time the *Borie*'s men came face to face with their enemy (I'm sure it was the first time for the Germans also). What a shock. The enemy weren't huge men with crew haircuts, wearing monocles and carrying short whips. They were, for the most part, frightened young men. When they recovered from their very close encounter with death and their natural apprehension about what would happen next, I'm sure they were just as surprised as we were to find that the enemy was just other young boys.

The able-bodied survivors climbed aboard pretty much on their own, most of them showing little or no emotion. The badly wounded were received on deck with much admiration. Although they required help to get on deck, which was beautifully provided by Kurz and Wenz at the waterline, and carefully assisted by caring men on deck, they did their best to control their emotions and pain.

They were greeted by sailors armed with Colt .45 pistols who, in turn, escorted them to an official greeter, Bill Schmalberger, boatswain's mate first class. Bill was, without a doubt, the best person for the assignment. He was big, intelligent, and a leader who handled problems with the proper mixture of discipline and compassion. He wasn't fluent in German, but he did know enough to understand a little, and he could read faces, so he did a wonderful job assigning locations for the prisoners. The *Borie* had just about a complete complement for the number of living spaces available so, what would we do with the sudden addition of forty-four men? Adding to the problem, they were a security risk and there were seven seriously wounded who needed immediate medical treatment. There were also four men with not so serious wounds. The able-bodied went to forward crew's compartment, officers to a cabin in the *Borie*'s officers' quarters, and the seriously wounded to the wardroom, where the dining room table was to be used for surgery.

The Germans posed little or no attitude problem as they came aboard. But of course, as with any group, some required different treatment from others. Bill knew just the right approach. I'm sure there were many stories, some funny, some sad, and some of just human interest. I remember only two of Bill's. One man stood waiting for Bill to talk to him, swaying back and forth. Bill happened to notice blood dripping to the deck, and he tore the back off the German's shirt. He found a huge bullet hole in the man's shoulder, yet he hadn't complained at all.

The only survivor who was a real pain in the ass was the captain, Adolf Graef. Unlike the other survivors, he was a caricature of the typical Nazi. Uninjured, he arrogantly marched up to Bill, without being summoned, and demanded to be taken to our commanding officer. Now devoid of compassion but loaded with passion, Bill, not calm and serene, screamed something like, "Get your ass out of here; you'll see the captain when and if he wants to." Graef seemed to get the point.

While Walter Kurz and Dick Wenz were still in the water, someone reported sighting a spread of five torpedoes passing just aft of the stern. That marksman was a lousy shot, missing a target that was dead in the water. Not wishing to improve his score, we ended our rescue operations and left the area. It was unfortunate, though, because there could have been more survivors of *U-664*. *U-664* normally carried a crew of four officers and fifty-six ratings, but we had picked up only forty-four. I was never able to ascertain the number of men aboard *U-664* at the time it was sunk. Walter Kurz said, "We sure took off like a Ford V-8 when the torpedoes were fired."

Under way again, the *Borie* searched for the "shooter." Finding nothing, she resumed station on the port bow of the *Card*. Then it was time to attend to the prisoners. The uninjured prisoners in the forward crew's compartment had to be guarded. There was only one exit from the compartment so that required only two men armed with submachine guns. If the prisoners wanted to use the head, they had to climb two ladders to get on deck and then walk aft about seventy yards. They couldn't be allowed to go alone, so a *Borie* man, armed with a Colt .45 caliber automatic pistol, escorted them to and from the head.

A friendly atmosphere developed after the Germans finally realized they weren't to be ill treated. Those men truly believed that New York had been bombed and that their submarine warfare had just about defeated the Allies. The group in the crew's quarters became content with their lot and were treated in a friendly fashion by their guards. Many were unhappy when they had to leave us to go on the *Card*.

Our medical officer, Lt. (jg) Walter F. Merscher, had come aboard in August 1943, so that was his first trip. He was instantly liked by all the men. Did you ever meet someone and know, right away, that that person could be a lifelong friend? That was the way I felt about Walter. Not long after he came aboard I had some problem and asked Dr. Merscher about it. He said, "Gee, Maher, I don't know." He then explained that one advantage of being a navy doctor was that he didn't need a bedside manner. He was my kind of doctor.

It was obvious to everyone when the wounded came on deck that they would need serious medical attention. Most, if not all, had been wounded by strafing with very large machine-gun bullets. The bullets were roughly three-quarters of an inch in diameter, and some of them exploded upon contact. Dr. Merscher went to work at once, setting up an emergency operating room (the officers' wardroom) and using the dining table as a surgical table. Assisted by Walter Kurz, he did magical tricks of surgery under the most demanding conditions. Among other things, he amputated the lower leg of one prisoner. He was already held in high esteem by the crew, but our respect for him now knew no bounds. As reports of his efforts trickled down to the prisoners, their growing respect for and gratitude to him could be felt by all and contributed to their desire to remain on the *Borie*. I heard (but didn't see) that the amputee gave, or at least offered, his Iron Cross to Dr. Merscher.

The U-boat officers (and maybe others) had been placed in the officers' living spaces. They were guarded by Selig Sirota, seaman second class, who was a new sailor. Selig was another one of those lovable Damon Runyan characters every ship has. Selig had been recently drafted and was near the maximum draft age, which made him unusually old (near thirty-eight) to hold the rating of S2/C. Most of our noncommissioned officers were in their early twenties. He had been a New York City taxi driver and talked and acted with all the mannerisms of one.

Selig was Jewish, could speak a little German (he said because of knowing Yiddish), and was foxy enough to keep the Germans from knowing that. All of them had claimed they didn't speak or understand English. Selig kept track of what went on and later reported what he knew, adding something like, "The old guy did pretty good, hey?"

Even though Selig bore the brunt of good-natured jokes, he showed patience and, in one case at least, pathos. The very seriously wounded were placed on stretchers before they were sent to the *Card*. A photographer on the *Card* took motion pictures of the entire operation of transferring the prisoners from the *Borie* to *Card*. A wounded German, strapped in a basket stretcher and obviously in great pain, as viewed on the film later, was being attended to by a *Borie* crewman: Selig. Selig was kneeling, patting the prisoner's head, but he suddenly stood up, walked off, then returned with a cup of water. Again kneeling and patting the man's head, he helped him drink the water. The unfortunate man probably never realized the irony of that act of kindness and compassion. In a few months Selig was again to show his fortitude.

While the *Borie* was occupied with *U-664*, the war went on. The *Barry* and *Goff* had three contacts, but one didn't count. It was a whale. The *Card* had its problems; it lost an Avenger that ditched when engine trouble

developed. The crew was picked up by the plane guard. Trouble not ending there, another Avenger was damaged while landing. The tail hook
missed the arresting gear, making the aircraft a missile, and the plane
smashed into a crash barrier, damaging the engine and propeller. The
plane was quickly repaired aboard the ship.

On August 10, it was decided to transfer the prisoners while the *Borie*
was taking on fuel. Refueling while under way is difficult enough, but
adding the transfer of personnel, some wounded, by high line, made the
job one great feat of seamanship. The seamanship was handled in great
fashion by boatswain's mates Bill Schmalberger and Walter Kurz and their
deck crew. Connecting to the oil hoses from the *Card,* dangerous and certainly not easy, was supervised by the "Oil King," Joe Kiszka, WT2c, and
done by his engineering gang. Joe was to lose his life in three months.

After the fuel hoses were connected and refueling commenced, a high-
line system was rigged. It was a rope and pulley combination that could
carry either a mail bag or a stretcher from the galley deckhouse of the
Borie across the water and up to the deck of the *Card,* a vertical distance of
about fifty feet. The ships were separated by about two hundred feet and
moving as fast as possible. Constant rolling of the vessels caused the high-
line to act like a slingshot; sometimes it was slack, then—zing, it would
snap taut. With the sea churning below, it was a dangerous method of
transportation, especially considering that the vehicle used to move the
prisoners was a closed mail bag.

Told to get ready to be moved to another ship, the prisoners showed
real concern. They were content to be aboard the *Borie* and didn't want to
go from the known to the unknown. Going was bad enough, but when
they saw they were to be sent to the *Card* by air mail, sealed in a bag, some
of them went ballistic. Many of them also were deathly afraid to go aboard
the carrier because they were convinced it was doomed to be sunk soon.
Great compassion and careful handling was shown to the wounded as they
were moved, strapped in metal stretchers. We thought it was hilarious to
watch the others as they were sealed in the canvas bags, then whisked
across the treacherous water, all the while going up and down like yo-yos.
There is an old saying that goes something like, "He who laughs at something should know what the hell he's laughing about" because we (*Borie*
sailors) were soon to recreate this funny scene as the star attraction.

Fueling finished and all the prisoners gone, *Borie* returned to its escort
station. I think the *U-664* operation was a valuable lesson for both the
Borie men and the Germans. Courage, honor, compassion, humor, and understanding were exhibited by both sides.

A wounded German survivor is "high-lined" from the galley deckhouse of the *Borie* to the flight deck of the *Card*. (Official U.S. Navy photograph)

Huff-Duff was still working. The damn thing never stopped. About the time we finished refueling, Huff-Duff radio traffic indicated submarines were in an area north of the Azores, islands northwest of Africa.

Sure enough, a submarine was sighted the next morning, August 11. Lt. (jg) Charles G. Hewitt, flying an Avenger bomber, and Ens. Jack H. Stewart, flying a Wildcat, spotted *U-525* cruising on the surface at about 15 miles. It was a 740-ton type VII-C, except it was fitted out as a supply boat rather than as an attack boat.

Stewart, at maximum diving speed, made a strafing run, watching his bullets explode along the deck and against the conning tower. No one was on deck. Possibly the crew had seen the *Card* aircraft, because it appeared to Hewitt that *U-525* was starting to submerge as he dropped his two bombs. Both bombs exploded close to the boat, on the port side, between the conning tower and the stern. For whatever reason, the stern came out of the water and *U-525* appeared to be diving.

Stewart made another strafing run, pulling up and circling above the submerging *U-525*. Although *U-525* was now under water, Stewart was

U-664 survivors on the hanger deck of the *Card.* The U-boat's captain, Kapitänleutant Adolf Graef, is the tall man fourth from the left in the front row.

able to see her, watching as Hewitt dropped his Fido. Stewart had a perfect seat for what followed. He saw the Fido hit the water, close to the vortex caused by the submerging sub, then, like a good, faithful hunting dog, turn towards its prey and head directly into it. Again, the usual large column of water blew into the air, signaling the end of *U-525.* All hands were lost as the U-boat went to the bottom.

Shortly thereafter, *Borie* received a message from the commander in chief of the Atlantic Fleet. Our group, *Card, Borie, Barry, Goff,* and VC Squadron 1, was honored with a "well done" from the Navy Department for the antisubmarine successes on the cruise. The score so far was four confirmed sunk, three probably sunk, and three damaged: Good Guys 10, Germans 0.

Continuing our cruise without further incident, we arrived in Casablanca on August 16, anchoring about 1900. The German prisoners were removed from the *Card,* and I'm sure that was a major disappointment for them since many thought we were heading for the United States.

You know, unless you have a heart of stone, you can't help but wonder what happened to the prisoners while on the *Card.* A member of the

Card crew kept a daily dairy (against the rules, but who cares now) called, "My Nine Cruises Aboard the USS *Card (CVE 11)*," by H. H. Babson. From that diary:

> While taking a shower this morning, six prisoners were washing up, they were young and didn't seem like such bad guys; According to the Master-at-arms they liked the ship and are giving no trouble at all; They are surprised at the good treatment they are receiving, same food, new shirts and dungarees, toilet articles, a cot and blankets; The wounded are getting along quite well except for one. His heart stopped and our doctor revived him; Two of the three officers harangued Captain Isbell and his executive officer.

Apparently Adolf was not only arrogant, but not too bright. He and his second officer were put in the brig on bread and water. One of their problems was that they didn't like being served by Negro waiters at the officers' wardroom table. I'm sure they found being served their sumptuous meals in a tin cup, on a tin plate, without a table and waiters, to be just magnificent.

Liberty didn't start until the next day, August 17. For some reason, going ashore didn't interest me that time. I thought about drinking a couple more bottles of the same wine I had had with my eggs last time, only to see what was wrong with it, of course. Then, thinking more about it, I realized that because we were anchored in the harbor, we could get ashore only in a small boat. I don't remember that I went ashore at all. If I did, I didn't do anything dumb because I always remember those things. I probably washed clothes, wrote letters, and read.

August 21 at 1000 we were off again, sailing in a northwesterly direction, probably headed towards the Azores. TG 21.14 was on the prowl again, but that direction had the benefit of terminating in the good old United States. Getting underway was exciting for all of us then because we knew what could happen. Also, after securing from special sea detail, we were informed that we had no convoy responsibility; the trip was to be just a search and destroy mission as we made our way home. What we didn't know, however, was that ComInCh, Tenth Fleet, had reported a concentration of submarines near the Azores.

On the afternoon of August 22, TG 21.14 went to general quarters. *Card*'s radar had picked up an unidentified aircraft. Being in range of land-based enemy bombers, Captain Isbell immediately launched five fighters (Wildcats), all of which headed out on an interception course. False alarm; it was an American B24 on a regular patrol.

USS *Card* refueling a destroyer at sea. This is one of the destroyer group TG 21.14, but not the *Borie.* (Courtesy of the National Archives)

We had a little excitement at 0230 on August 24. Sound contact: echoes from an object between us and the *Card. Borie* made a depth charge attack, dropping four depth bombs with no obvious results. I doubt there had been a sub. If one had been able to penetrate our protection area that far, it would have launched torpedoes long before we found it.

On August 25, all of the tin cans refueled, which pretty much used up a whole day. Every time we refueled, at least on the *Borie,* a tableau unfolded. One of the big advantages of duty on a carrier was that many of the niceties of life were available. The *Card* had an old fashioned ice cream parlor, similar to those found in small towns of the day. You don't think a sailor would say ice cream parlor. Hell, if he did that everyone would know what he was talking about, so sailors called this ship's store, and also ice cream, "gedunk." The first time we refueled from the *Card,* one of our guys called up to the men lining the flight deck, "Hey, how about sending us some ice cream?" (During fueling operations, men always lined the deck of both ships, calling and shouting to each other.)

Many of the *Card* sailors rushed to get small cups of ice cream and throw them down to the *Borie* crew. An instant Keystone Cops movie evolved. The *Borie* men scrambled, bumping into each other, and knocking one another down. The funniest of all was when a wave came over the bow at the same time a cup arrived. Sometimes three or four men would be fighting for cups when a large wave would hit them, knocking them on their fannies and sliding them along until they hit the edge; all the while the men were trying to grab the cup before it went over the side. The first time I'm sure the *Card* sailors gave the *Borie* sailors ice cream out of the goodness of their hearts. After that I'm not so sure, especially since the bow became the main target.

August 27: Contact! Lieutenant (jg) Hogan, again searching his designated area, came across a submarine fully surfaced. After reporting his contact, Hogan charged in for an attack on *U-508* (type IXC U-boat). Because *U-508* had been alert, Hogan's Avenger came under heavy attack, which didn't change his plan. Armed with one five-hundred-pound bomb and a Fido, he attacked from the stern, but Kapitänleutnant Georg Staats, the CO of *U-508,* was good. Just before Hogan dropped his bomb, *U-508* made a sharp turn to port, followed by another turn to starboard. Hogan's bomb missed. He had to reduce his airspeed to drop his Fido, but when he did drop the Fido in the swirl left by *U-508,* the sub was too deep and it got away.

Upon his return to the *Card,* Hogan reported to Captain Isbell and the flight officer on the bridge. He was heard to say that he thought the sub had seen him at the same time it was spotted by Hogan. That's why there wasn't enough time to even damage the sub. He really was very upset about missing and was heard to say, "God only knows when one will ever run into another one again." Hey, he had already scored on *U-664.*

Hogan had radioed to *Card* for assistance, standard procedure, before he attacked *U-508.* So while Hogan was making his bomb run, a team of one Avenger and two Wildcats was racing to join the attack. By the time they were in the area, Hogan and *U-508* were gone. But, as so often happens, fate entered the scene. A different boat, *U-847* (type IXD₂ U-boat), was there on the surface. *U-847* was a 1,610-ton transport submarine designed to carry critical war supplies from the Far East to Germany. For comparison, an attack submarine such as *U-508* was 740 tons.

The leader of the attack team, Lt. (jg) Ralph W. Long, in the Avenger, ordered his fighter pilots, Lt. (jg) Frederick M. Roundtree and Ensign Stewart, to strafe *U-847,* which they did. Roundtree went in first, with Stewart not far behind. They both encountered fire from machine guns on the conning tower without getting hit, but on each of the fighter passes a man was seen to go down.

U-847 suddenly stopped firing and started to dive. As soon as Round-tree and Stewart were clear, Lieutenant Long descended to let Fido off the leash. Fido hit just a little to the starboard and forward of the now-familiar swirl. Seconds later there was a large disturbance in the water and oil came to the surface. However, that disturbance was minor compared to what followed. Long, overhead, saw the huge flash of an underwater explosion that lasted less than a second and was the size of a football field. What remained of *U-847* was on its way to the bottom.

Reading from the diary of a *Card* sailor: "August 29, Captain Isbell was heard to say that our score is now five subs sunk and five subs damaged and that he would sure like to beat the score of the *Bogue* and her 'hunter-killer' group." The sailor went on to record: "If the Germans don't run out of submarines, we might be able to pull ahead of the *Bogue*."

On August 31 word was passed from Captain Isbell that ComInCh had issued another "well done" to TG 21.14. Two commendations in one cruise was an almost unheard of feat. Captain Isbell also updated the score to six positive sinkings, four probables, and one possible. At 2200 a de-stroyer sound man (not *Borie*) heard sounds of running torpedoes, and at the same time a *Card* lookout reported two torpedo wakes passing astern of *Card*. A course change was made for TG 21.14. The destroyer inves-tigated but couldn't make contact and returned to station. That doesn't sound like much, but to be awakened by the bong, bong, bong of general quarters; hearing, "All hands man your battle stations"; and then arriving on deck to find we were under torpedo attack did absolutely nothing for our nerves. It didn't help us sleep either.

September 1 brought another alert. Bong, bong, bong. "All hands man your battle stations!" 2200 again. *Barry* got a solid sound contact, close aboard, and dropped eleven depth charges that brought debris, oil, and bubbles to the surface. There was so much garbage that Captain Isbell, certain that *Barry* had a kill, radioed the Tenth Fleet headquarters to in-form them of the sinking.

It was the last submarine incident of that cruise. We proceeded toward home without a problem. That is, unless you classify a destroyer in a hur-ricane a problem.

We headed west for several days on what we thought was a course to Norfolk. The aircraft went out on their daily search missions but didn't get any sub contacts. That was fine with us. We had all the time in the world to ourselves, except for our daily work (0800–1600) and our daily eight hours of watch duty.

We noticed that the sea was getting increasingly rough; about September 6, the waves started to hammer us about—nothing we couldn't handle yet. But we did notice that sea water began to splash over the flight deck of the carrier occasionally, and green water washed over our bow. The new spray shield that had been welded to the deck, just forward of gun no. 1, while we were in the Brooklyn Navy Yard, helped keep the deck from being completely awash.

The wind and the speed and size of the waves rapidly increased, and life aboard became more and more uncomfortable. There were no flight operations that day, not that it made any difference in the war effort. All submarines would stay as deep as necessary to get a smooth ride; if they stayed at periscope level there was also the danger of inadvertently popping to the surface.

More and higher bow waves crashed over the deck, and the green water started to hit higher on the bridge. Stan Hull and I were a helmsman team. We shared four-hour watches when we would each steer the ship for two hours and stand lookout watches on the outer edge of the navigational bridge for two hours. We alternated watches, one hour at the helm, one hour on lookout, one hour helm, and one hour on lookout. *Borie,* being an older ship, had a large helm, between three and four feet in diameter. Turning the wheel pulled cables that ran the length of the ship, from the wheel back to the steering engine. The engine moved the rudder when the wheel was turned. Up to then we were able to do quite well steering, but it was getting more difficult. Especially getting more uncomfortable was standing lookout in a "bucket" mounted on the side of the bridge. The increasing wind pelted the rain against our faces, harder and harder. It didn't make any difference what we wore; we got soaked to the skin. I hated that duty, particularly at night under those conditions. As I stood there, the ship started to roll farther and farther until it seemed as if my face would touch the raging, tumultuous sea. Thankfully, just as I started to panic, the ship seemed to say, "Don't worry, Maher" and slowly begin its roll to the other side, which didn't bother me. The roar of the wind was so loud and forceful I knew that if I were washed over the side no one would hear me call for help. Up to then I was okay, but I knew things were going to get worse, much worse, before they got better.

Eating was a problem. Later in the war most, if not all, ships served meals at a central place, putting the entire meal on metal trays. Since *Borie* had been around since the elegant days of Tom Jefferson, we were served home style, getting our food from serving dishes or pans. We passed the food down the length of the table, each man putting his serving directly onto a dinner plate. In that weather, when the ship rolled past a certain point everything went to hell. If I held on to my coffee cup, my plate slid in two directions; if I held on to the plate, the cup slid across the table and fell onto the deck. Suddenly we hit the first really big boomer. Coming from the side of the bow, it caused the bow to rise sharply and take a big roll at the same time. Neatness counts, but not more than survival; all hands grabbed the nearest support to save their fannies. Crash, splash— we lost most of our dinnerware as everything slid aft, off the table, to become a pile of busted junk. Just prior to that we had heard stuff crashing in the galley. Now we heard the cook screaming and swearing. Everything he had been cooking was on the galley deck! We knew we wouldn't get any more cooked meals during that storm. We didn't have enough plates to go around anyhow.

The next day we were in a full-fledged hurricane-force storm. It was time for concern. That wasn't our first such storm, but believe me, it didn't get any easier with experience, especially for our type of destroyer (flush deck). Being 314 feet long by about 30 feet wide at the widest part, *Borie* fit neatly, but not comfortably, in between waves sometimes as high as forty feet. In a hurricane, green water smashed over the bow, often whacking the bridge windows, and huge waves came over the deck the entire length of the ship. It was impossible to get food from the galley, across a wide open deck, and down two ladders when the intense rolling and pitching of the ship was added to the unforgiving, dangerous waves. Our formal dinners now consisted of apples in a washtub, hanging by lines, and a large coffee pot, also hanging by lines. It wasn't all bad. As you can imagine, it was fun to see how much coffee—if any—you could get in the cup as you poured.

What I dreaded most was going to the head. A cable was strung from all the way forward, along both outside edges of the main deck. Sliding strap hangers were available to grasp for safety while we went both forward and aft. The situation was dangerous with the path running so close to the water's edge. At the very best, we were sure to get blasted by a heavy wave, and there was danger of being washed over the top of the low lifelines.

Except for working on deck, which was impossible, everything went on nearly as usual. My wheel watches (steering the ship) naturally went on, but not as usual. The wind during that storm reached more than seventy miles per hour at times, and for a few days it never was less than fifty miles per hour. Captain Hutchins had the tough responsibility of maintaining his position with respect to the *Card*.

My turn on the wheel was from noon to 1600. Green water smashed into the windows of the bridge in front of me. I couldn't keep from ducking my head as each wave roared over the bow, over gun no. 1. Most of it hit the bridge directly in front of my face, but some went even higher and sprayed the flying bridge. You've seen pictures of a deep sea fisherman with a sailfish on his line. The fish comes straight out of the water, twists and turns, and then smashes down again. That was the *Borie* then. A "line" came from the clouds to the very bow of the ship, and as a wave, possibly forty feet high, rolled in, our bow rose almost straight out of the water. As we reached the crest of the wave, *Borie* changed direction to become parallel with the wave just before we slid and jolted to the bottom of the next wave. We were about twenty degrees off course. I spun the helm full rudder, trying to get back on course, but when the ship reached the crest and started down again, the screws and rudder came out of the water. We could feel the ship quiver and shake, and before the screws and rudder were back where they belonged, the ship pointed to wherever nature called. That happened over and over again—full opposite rudder, hit the wave, a groaning ship, and more terror. By the time Stan relieved me, I was exhausted, both physically and mentally. When he relieved me he said that he saw the *Goff* riding on top of a wave with the underwater sound dome exposed.

I went out into the driving rain, roaring winds, and blasting seas, and for the longest time I didn't even get a glimpse of *Goff* or *Barry*. We must have been going down when they were coming up. It was reassuring when, every now and then, I spotted the *Card*. I knew then we weren't alone.

Henry Babson wrote in his diary:

Today we are in the middle of a hurricane. . . . It's a lot of fun for me and I'm enjoying it. The swells are as high as the ship (about twice as high as *Borie*) and, when you look at them, it looks like a big steep hill with us between two big ones. . . . We are taking a beating like never before . . . this is the roughest the ship has ever seen but she is doing good and riding it out. All the planes are lashed down on the hanger deck and so is everything else that could move. The tin cans must be the ones that are suffering, we don't see them half of the time. They are farther away than normal, riding out the storm as we are. Some times they are visible but most of the times they are not as the waves are really huge. About the only time that we see them is when we are on top of a huge wave at the same time. . . . We had quite a downfall in the mess hall today. While eating, all the mess tables were lashed down and all the legs gave way together. All the trays, silverware and everything else, crew included, ended up on deck. Most of the food ended up on the men. What a mess. From now on, until the storm dies down, we are only going to have sandwiches and coffee. We are not too certain about the coffee. . . . The wind is still blowing at more than fifty miles an hour. . . . Most of the men who are not on watch are in their bunks as there isn't much that can be done on the ship in this kind of weather.

Boy! I sure wish we (*Borie* crew) could have had it as good as they did. We weren't even sure of sandwiches. Stan and I went on watch again, from midnight to 0400. After maybe an hour or so of sleep, we were rousted out of our bunks and sent into the same lousy conditions. I knew things hadn't improved when I walked three times as far from port to starboard as I did going aft towards the bridge. I had the first hour at the helm. I thought things had been bad on the last watch and couldn't get worse, but shortly into the later watch, the gyro compass suddenly went out. I had to switch to steering by the magnetic compass. If you have a compass in your car it's magnetic. You must have noticed that when you make a turn or hit a bump, the compass goes wild, and by the time it settles down, you've forgotten you were using it. It was hard enough to steer magnetic in good weather, but in that storm, it was impossible. I would get the order, "Come left to 270." I would reply, "Left to 270, sir." When the bow was swinging between 250 and 300 I would lie. "Steady on 270, sir." The OD's reply, "Very well," without looking, told me that he didn't know what he was doing either. When Stan Hull relieved me at 0100, I told him how lucky he was to have the opportunity to steer by magnetic compass. His watch was more of the same, and whenever necessary he and the OD lied to each other also. I relieved Stan at 0300, happy that only one more hour remained of the watch and believing that things couldn't get any worse. I was into my watch by maybe five minutes when the steering wheel jammed! I couldn't budge it in either direction. Keeping the ship more or less on course while steering magnetic was extremely difficult, even with a working helm. But now the ship was a free-floating cork. And as you can imagine, all hell broke loose. Stan was ordered to go aft and man the emergency steering wheel on the galley deckhouse, receiving

course information by phone. With the deck awash and rolling and pitching severely, Stan had to make his way, in the dark, a distance of about half
the length of a football field. There was also the very real danger he could
be washed over the side. Taking the wheel, he attempted to get the ship
on course. Slipping and sliding, he was soon on his fanny. Standing on a
brass deck, awash with rain, he couldn't maintain his footing. Our bos'un
mate of the watch, Oakley Hamilton, went back, with the same risks,
and tied Hull to stanchions on both sides, keeping him firmly in place. At
least now he was able to keep *Borie* on course, more or less, with a little
bit of lying.

Next day we were on watch again, 1200–1600. Same weather, same
problems. Even though we were using the emergency steering wheel, the
ship's rudder was still moved by the steering engine located below deck
at the fantail (stern). In heavy weather or at high speeds, the fantail was
always under water, some of which leaked into the steering engine room.
The steering engine room was kept clear of water by suction from the
after engine room. Suddenly the engineers of the after engine room reported they had lost suction, and the steering engine had to be turned off
because of the water accumulating.

That was it. We were now at the end of our steering rope—the last
method of keeping the ship on course. Two huge wheels in the steering
engine room connected in tandem, directly to the rudder. Two men, one
looking forward and one looking aft, could move the rudder by turning
those wheels. Stan and I went down below; I took the wheel that faced
forward, and Stan, wearing the phones from the bridge, faced aft. Oh,
what fun it was being down in that hole, water up to our hips, and literally
steering the ship by hand. We managed to do a pretty good job of steering
in spite of all the problems, but I must admit that our first efforts looked a
little bit like a Laurel and Hardy movie. Stan had the phone on and would
say, "Right 20 degrees." I would turn clockwise and Stan would turn clockwise. The wheel didn't move. After I called him a dummy several times he
said, "You take the phone." After a few more Laurel and Hardys, we got
the system working. By the time our next watch arrived, the storm had
decreased to baby size. A rag had jammed the steering cables, and another
rag had stuffed the vacuum lines to the steering engine room.

Henry Babson's diary read:

Last night and all of today was really rough and we all knew that we
were in a good storm . . . there were many waves that broke over the

Here I am on the after deckhouse. The emergency steering wheel is in the background, and the dark-colored deck is brass—slippery when wet.

flight deck . . . the waves were looking like mountains sometimes. . . . We had no real meals today, other than sandwiches for breakfast, dinner and supper. . . . I can't get over how rough it has been and I do feel sorry for the guys on the tin cans. . . . The wind was strong earlier today and was blowing across the flight deck at sixty-eight miles per hour. . . . we are only averaging about two miles per hour in actual distance traveled towards home.

September 9, 1943, the storm finally subsided, and we cruised under sunny skies through a glasslike sea. We were finally making normal headway towards Norfolk. Everyone was inspecting and cleaning up or repairing the mess caused by the clobbering we took. Believe me, the destroyer crews would much rather take their chances with fighting submarines than go through one of those storms. However, I was soon to rue the day I had that thought.

September 10, 1943, we arrived in Norfolk. What a satisfying cruise! It was so different from our convoy duty, and I had no doubt that because of the efforts of TG 21.14 the war would be over sooner. But not soon enough.

Even Norfolk looked good after Casablanca and several days of a hurricane. Once we got used to the facts of liberty in Norfolk and knew what we weren't going to find—friendly company—it wasn't all that bad. We managed to stay off the lawns of the locals on our way to some decent restaurants, movies, and maybe even a bar now and then. Allegri, Cliff, and I had lots of work, getting our equipment back in working order. All of our electrical and optical instruments were mounted on our main battery, directly exposed to the weather. They were supposed to be waterproof, and they were for the type of waves one normally expected. But after being zonked by miniature tidal waves for days, all bets were off. The instruments had been filled with salt water, even though we had used the best waterproof material available. The gunsight telescopes didn't fare a lot better. Everything had to be opened up, washed with fresh water, dried, tested, and sealed again. That pretty much used up all of the working time we had for the two weeks or so we stayed in Norfolk. After work, Jim and I probably went ashore most of the time, if for nothing else, just to get a decent meal and get off the ship.

Doris remained in Newark at her family's home since none of us had any idea how long we would remain in port. I did think of calling

Stan Hull and me, both as seamen first class.

Admiral King, ComInCh, Tenth Fleet, to ask if he knew anything. I really didn't have that thought; I just like to talk navy talk sometimes. It sounds so, well, navy.

September 25, 1943, off we went again. Early that morning we heard the order, "All hands, man your special sea detail." Special sea detail manned, we were ready to take in our lines from the dock. One forlorn sailor on the dock, in dress blues and sea bag at his side, waited for us to go. Only we couldn't go unless that lonely sailor let go our lines, which he did. As we started to move away from the dock he waved, and I, sadly, waved back to my shipmate, Stan Hull. For the first time since boarding the *Borie* I really felt the meaning of the word *shipmate*. Friends come and go, but shipmates are forever.

His friends were happy for him because he had been assigned to torpedo school with further orders for new construction—an assignment we all had been trying to get ever since Pearl Harbor. I knew I would miss "Sea Gull". I was in line behind him when we got our first immunization shots, and our service numbers are the same except for the last. Stan's last number was two; mine was three. I was in line behind him when we got our uniforms. We were assigned the same watch section and had stayed together until that day. We even both got seasick for the first time, within a half hour of each other. Yes, I would miss him. I wondered, as I watched him grow smaller, if I would ever see him again. I would, and I still do.

At eight A.M. TG 21.14 steamed out of Hampton Roads, Virginia, headed for, we later found out, Bermuda. I felt lucky about that trip since we just missed starting our mission on my birthday. We will soon see if I was justified in feeling lucky.

As we headed for Bermuda, the weather was beautiful—warm summer breezes and a sea calm as glass. Was that a good omen? Was Mother Nature trying to atone for nearly killing us a few weeks ago? I would like that. We heard that we would be supporting a huge convoy called *UGS-19*. I hadn't figured out the east-west convoy naming system as yet, but we knew that our task would be to sweep the seas ahead of *UGS-19* rather than be an integral unit of the convoy. That was in compliance with Captain Isbell's plan that was used on the successful mission from Casablanca to Norfolk. *Card*'s original composite Squadron One had been replaced with *Bogue*'s veteran VC-9 group. We knew we would be in good hands with the new "fly boys."

We saw the convoy that day, and no matter how many times we saw the majestic sight of ships, stretching from horizon to horizon, peacefully steaming on a placid sea, it became no less awesome. "Stars and Stripes Forever" seemed to explode in my mind, and once again I knew what I was fighting for. Proud to be American? You tell me. We probably wouldn't see *UGS-19* once we were on our sortie, but we knew why we were there and were glad to be there.

On day two, September 27, things seemed to be going almost too well. Still beautiful summer weather and a glassy sea with flying fish darting about. By now I knew how to spot them, and it gave me devious pleasure to say to a new recruit, "Whadja mean, you can't see the flying fish?" Of course I didn't tell the poor guy that it took me about a week before I saw one.

About 0900 on September 27 we sighted Bermuda, and I must say it was the prettiest island I have ever seen, with white sandy beaches, outlined by beautiful green grass and surrounded by crystal clear water. We anchored at about 1300, but for the life of me I can't remember if we got liberty or not. I know the *Card* sailors went ashore, but my gut feeling is that *Borie* sailors did not. Being a nice guy, I'll tell you why. The next morning an announcement was made over the loudspeaker system that the *Card* would not be allowed any more liberties in Bermuda for at least one year. Why? Most of the sailors not only got drunk as skunks (medium drunk) but also got involved in fights. I knew that our crew would not have become involved in something as ungentlemanly as fighting while they were guests of a friendly country. Not in that short span of time anyway. If you remember, it took us two days to be kicked out of St. Petersburg, but that was different I think; it was our own country.

Anyway we were in Bermuda less than a full day, leaving at 0900 on September 28 and remaining in sight of convoy *UGS-19* for the whole day. It was kind of nice and gave us the feeling of being a big brother. But next day, September 29, we were out on our own, with no convoy in sight. We were again operating in the "get 'em before they get us" mode. Our planes were out on patrol for the first time since leaving Norfolk, so maybe there had been a Huff-Duff contact. I don't know; Hutch wouldn't tell me. In fact his attitude gave me the impression I had better get off his bridge.

Day six and everything was still quiet. We waited for the other shoe to drop. There were a couple of airplane accidents, which did tend to raise the adrenalin, but then any time aircraft were taking off or being recovered, the whole task force had to be alert for any emergency. One of the F4F fighters ran out of gas while in the landing circle. He crashed about four miles away and was picked up by *Goff* or *Barry*. It was a good thing the plane was a fighter and not an Avenger with its three-man crew. It went down so fast that at least one man would have gone down with it. Another F4F crashed on the flight deck while landing. Fortunately the pilot was uninjured, except for his pride, but the whole landing undercarriage was smashed, and the propeller carved a big chunk out of the wooden flight deck.

At last the other shoe dropped. Captain Isbell passed the word to our bridge that ComInCh had informed him of a concentration of submarines, to the northeast of us, about eight hundred miles distant. We changed our heading to 064 degrees and steamed toward the area.

The captain let it be known that because of the *Borie*'s experience with *U-664* there would be no rescue operations for U-boat survivors. He didn't want to risk losing a destroyer or endangering his carrier.

Day seven passed as we moved closer to the hunting grounds. The destroyers were sniffing as we moved along but had located no game as yet. The planes were out all day but nothing was sighted. We received some additional intelligence. The size of the group was estimated at about six boats. It could make quite a nice surprise party, surprise being the key word.

By day eight, the destroyers needed to be refueled. After we connected up and started to take on fuel, the usual ice cream tossing game began. It was even funnier that time as there was a twenty-five knot wind in addition to the mandatory waves breaking over the bow. There were a lot more wet fannies and near misses as men slid into the lifelines while trying to catch the elusive ice cream cups. According to the diary from the *Card*, one guy had an exciting time. He fell over the side, in between his ship and the *Card*. Fortunately he drifted down the middle and was picked up by the following destroyer. I don't know if that was a work-related accident or if it happened when he slipped trying to catch ice cream. I had decided a long time ago that I really didn't like ice cream that much.

On the ninth day we saw Flores Island, a part of the Azores chain, so now we had an idea where we were. A damned likely spot to find submarines, but not that day.

Day ten, October 4 at 1030, Lieutenant (jg) Stearns, flying his Avenger, saw what could be a submarine, at a distance of about fifteen miles. He informed his crew of the possible sighting, but went absolutely nuts when he got closer, crying out, "There are four of them!" Now, finding four U-boats on the surface was a big break, to say the least. But, and it is a big but, one of them was *U-460* (type XIV U-boat), a so-called milch cow. Those boats were 1,688 tons, designed to carry 432 tons of oil, torpedoes, ammunition, and food to replenish the attack submarines. The obvious advantage was that the attack subs could remain on patrol longer.

When the hunter-killer groups first saw action, and their pilots saw their first subs, every submarine sighted was a milch cow to the excited, inexperienced young men. The truth is that Germany built only ten of them, and *U-460* was one of only three left as of that date. Of the other two, *U-488* was sunk on April 26, 1944, and *U-490* was sunk on June 12, 1944. By comparison, Germany built approximately 660 VIIC boats. One of those false milch cow sightings was to cause the *Borie* a little trouble in a few short weeks. And I do mean trouble.

U-460 had just finished fueling *U-264* (type VIIC U-boat) and was moving into position to fuel *U-422* (another VIIC). The third VIIC was waiting her turn. All four were in a group, about 500 yards in diameter and steaming slowly to the northwest. Naturally, Stearns sent a radio contact report, but the transmission was bad and Isbell knew only about a contact, not that there were four prizes.

Vroom. Vroom. Vroom. A TBF Avenger (armed with four depth bombs) and two Wildcats streaked to the aid of their fellow pilot. Stearns circled at 5,000 feet before he attacked; then, in a steep dive, he went at the center of the group.

Milch cows were under orders to dive when attacked and not be dead heroes. However, *U-460*'s commander, Kapitänleutnant Heinrich Schnoor, got into an argument with *U-264*'s Kapitänleutnant Paul Hartwig about who would dive first. Neither boat submerged.

Now the U-boats were in real trouble. As Stearns bore in, all four subs started firing at him, but he kept on, dropping one 500-pound bomb in between the *U-460* and the *U-264*. Unfortunately, little damage was done to the U-boats, but fortunately no damage was done to Stearns. However, the four boats stayed on the surface and tried to maneuver around each other. Stearns decided to wait for assistance before he dropped his Fido.

Lt. (jg) D. E. Weigle arrived at 1032 expecting to find only one U-boat. Once he spotted the four boats, he informed Captain Isbell. Three Avengers on search patrol were immediately vectored to the area. Just to make sure, *Card* launched five more Avengers and two Wildcats, making a total of ten warplanes on the way to join Weigle and Stearns in the fray.

U-455, seeing Weigle's Avenger coming in, submerged just before two Wildcats (Lt. [jg] Elbert S. Heim and Lt. [jg] David O. Puckett) arrived. The two Wildcats dove directly at the group of boats for a strafing attack. The three remaining boats returned fire, setting up a formidable area of flak. The Wildcats flew through the fire. Heim got through untouched, but Puckett was hit several times. However, the planes' fifty-caliber bullets also took their toll, and the antiaircraft fire subsided.

U-422 submerged leaving *U-264* and *U-460* (the milch cow) on the surface. The attacking Americans assigned an Avenger to each submarine, with Wildcats going in first, strafing to reduce antiaircraft fire. Weigle's Avenger, following Puckett's Wildcat, started his bombing run. Weigle decided also to use his .50-caliber wing guns. Instead of pressing the gun trigger, he accidentally pressed the bomb release switch, dropping all four of his depth bombs. That wouldn't have been all that bad except he dropped them more than two football fields short.

Stearns, ready for a run on *U-460,* saw it submerge. Quickly changing direction, he attacked *U-264,* which was also diving. Arriving at his drop point he couldn't see *U-264.* Not to be undone, he chose to go back after *U-460,* which had been badly damaged by the continuous strafing of Heim and Puckett. Much too late, Schnoor started to dive, and Stearns, dropping his landing gear to lose speed, was able to track along *U-460'*s underwater wake. Dropping his acoustic torpedo (Fido) from about 200 feet, he saw it hit a short distance ahead of the boat. Stearns saw Fido turn sharply and watched the typical swelling disturbance seen after the explosion of a depth bomb. Mounds of oil, discolored water, and human debris floated to the surface; it was obvious that another milch cow had left the U-boat fleet forever. Puckett and Stearns were awarded the Navy Cross (navy's highest award) for their part in the action. That was the second time for Stearns.

This same day, another Avenger pilot on patrol spotted four "submarines" and sent a quick radio report to *Card:* "Send help." Not waiting for assistance, the pilot barreled in and dropped his depth charges. A few minutes later he cancelled his call for reinforcements, sheepishly reporting he had made an attack on four neutral, unarmed whales.

Remember *U-422?* The captain had left the party that morning, deciding he would be better off traveling alone. Late the same afternoon, he surfaced a few miles from where he had left *U-460* (now sunk) and *U-264.* The captain probably thought that the area was clear, but it wasn't. Directly above him, in scattered cloud cover, were Lt. (jg) Stewart B. Holt (Avenger) and Ens. Joseph D. Horn (Wildcat). Horn started strafing almost at once and continued firing all the way down, crossing *U-422* at about fifty feet. His tracer bullets could be seen smacking all around the conning tower. The U-boat dived, but Holt was so close to the Wildcat that his Fido hit the water only seconds after the submarine went under the surface. As with other successful Fido attacks, a column of water arose from the surface, soon followed by oil and wreckage. *U-422* was no longer a threat to Allied shipping.

Day eleven we just pounded the waves.

On day twelve, according to the quartermaster, our task group was traveling around in circles with ever increasing radii. Toward the end of the day, a course was set for the location of a reported wolf pack. It seemed to be getting colder.

The next day, day thirteen, we proceeded on course with aircraft being launched and recovered. The weather had been rotten—cold, windy, and occasionally foggy. What surprised me was that the *Card* had continued with air operations in spite of the weather. It was difficult enough to land those planes on that postage stamp even under good conditions.

It happened at dusk, with scattered rain squalls and fog, when the last four planes returned from patrol. Three came aboard without incident, at least from what we could see. The fourth, an Avenger piloted by Ens. C. H. Goodfield, was waved off because of a bad approach. He circled, and while he was still about five hundred yards from the ship, his plane suddenly spun into the ocean. He crashed quite close to *Borie* and we could see the pilot pulling on the canopy. Only one crew member got out, and we assumed it was the pilot. So did the people on the *Card.* The gunner, presumed lost, had a brother on the ship, and you can imagine the brother's feelings when he believed the gunner had gone down with the Avenger. The survivor was picked up by the plane guard, but it wasn't the pilot; it was the gunner. Despair turned to elation, but even that must have been hard to handle because two men had been lost, one being the pilot, who usually was the one to escape. We all felt the loss.

Even though the weather remained lousy, flight operations went on, but with no enemy contacts. We nosed about for a few days and at one time were only about seven hundred miles from England. That was a far piece from the Azores and the Bay of Biscay, the usual hunting grounds. Not that it made a lot of difference because the weather had been rough and foggy. If it hadn't been for radar, the high commands would have had to call off the war for a while.

No one called the war off. TG 21.14 found that out on October 12, after reports that another fueling rendezvous had been detected. The area for refueling was about six hundred miles north of the Azores. In spite of drizzle, fog, and very rough seas, *Card*'s planes went searching. My hat goes off to those guys who risked their lives, and knew it, just by going up in the air in that weather. Just before noon, Lieutenant (jg) Balliett's radioman saw a submarine, *U-488* (type XIV U-boat), surfacing. Balliett went in preparing for a Fido attack, but seeing the boat was fully on the surface, he had to switch to a bombing attempt. As he climbed to set up his depth bombs, *U-488* submerged again. Switching the attack mode once more, Balliett dropped his Fido. It missed and *U-488* got away. That was *U-488*'s lucky day; only a few hours later Lieutenant (jg) Fowler found it, also dropping a Fido that missed.

On the afternoon of October 12, Ensign Doty spotted *U-731* (type VIIC U-boat) on the surface through hazy visibility. He circled it a couple of times at one thousand feet and should have been detected but he wasn't. He climbed to about two thousand feet, still undetected. The Germans should have at least heard the engines while he climbed, but they didn't. In fact, they were oblivious to his presence until his bomb exploded about 175 feet away. They immediately sent up a barrage of antiaircraft fire. Doty, expecting and hoping that they would submerge, circled the boat. *U-731* stayed on the surface, so Doty started strafing to force them down. Instead, they tried to get away. About a half hour after the initial attack, Lieutenant (jg) Holt arrived in his Avenger. Zooming right in at the bow and receiving no antiaircraft fire, he dropped a 500-pound bomb. His bomb overshot *U-731* by almost a football field. Another player suddenly arrived in the form of Ensign Hodgson, flying an Avenger. Ignoring the heavy gunfire he was flying through, Hodgson dropped four bombs that exploded along the port side of *U-731*. With three bombers on the attack, *U-731* decided to dive. Doty dropped a Fido just as the boat went under the surface, causing a small column of water to rise. Since Fidos explode only when they hit an object, it was assumed that *U-731* was hit and destroyed. It wasn't. Although badly damaged, it managed to get back to base and was repaired. However, it didn't survive long after repairs, being sunk in May 1944.

Things sure were happening again, and on October 13 they started early. At 0800, Lieutnant (jg) Fowler snagged *U-378* (type VIIC U-boat) on the surface, and after receiving a flak shower, went in on a bombing attack. He pressed the release switch, but the bomb didn't release. As he climbed out, the boat submerged; Fowler, in an excellent exhibition of his flying skill, dropped an acoustic torpedo (Fido) ahead of the sub. It missed. (*U-378* would be sunk later by another hunter-killer group, the *Core* group, on October 20.)

Another Avenger was sent to assist Fowler, piloted by Lieutenant Commander Avery, but by the time he got to the area it was clear of any U-boats. Avery remained in the general area, hoping that *U-378* might surface again. He caught a U-boat on the surface, but it wasn't *U-378*. It was *U-402* (type VIIC U-boat), commanded by Korvettenkapitän Baron Siegfried von Forstner. The sea was still pretty rough; waves were crashing over the bow and conning tower, and Avery, seeing that, believed the boat was diving. He prepared his Fido and went straight in. Realizing that *U-402* wasn't diving, he maintained his dive and strafed the deck. The sub returned the fire, but not before Avery had started to pull up to gain altitude. The Avenger circled at a distance, off the bow, on the chance that the sub would go down, giving Avery a chance to use his Fido. Then, fate again entered the picture.

While keeping an eye on Avery and, probably, deciding whether or not to dive, von Forstner was shocked by the sudden explosion of a bomb. His crew had failed to see Ens. Barton C. Sheela coming in, diving at the stern, to drop a 500-pound bomb. The bomb exploded a short distance away. The boat dove so rapidly that the stern came out of the water before it went under.

That was exactly what Avery had been waiting and wishing for. Being set up for a Fido attack, he pushed full throttle to get close and then maneuvered so that he dropped his Fido less than a minute after the conning tower was under the water. It was a successful attack. Explosion, debris, and discolored water were seen. There was no doubt that Squadron VC-9 had scored another kill.

What a day! And the day wasn't over. Lt. (jg) H. E. Fryatt, on afternoon patrol with his Avenger, caught another submarine on the surface. He wasted no time, going right at it against heavy machine gun fire, some of which hit. Fryatt dropped a 500-pound bomb close aboard the conning tower, and the boat started to submerge. In spite of his damaged plane, he quickly came about and released his Fido. That time there were no indications of damage so he headed home.

It was the custom of *Card* to recover aircraft from the last patrol of the day at about sunset. That action took place at about 1700, so when Fryatt reached the *Card* the other airplanes were also returning. Bad news for Fryatt. When he entered the landing circle he discovered he couldn't lower his right wheel. He was told to circle the carrier while the other planes landed. That made sense, but conditions started to change. It was getting dark, the sea was visibly getting rougher, and Fryatt had to worry about gasoline. What happened later had a great impact on me, so I remember the dramatic events vividly. After fifty years the exact words might not be the same, but the drama as it unfolded is, I believe, quite accurate.

Don't forget, all of us could hear the voice transmissions. Equally important to remember, by now the names of those pilots were familiar to all of us, and we agonized with them while they were out on patrol. The word went around the ship that Fryatt had big problems, and I'm sure the word passed around the other tin cans also. All men who weren't busy soon had their eyes glued to the carrier deck and had prayers in their hearts.

TOWARD MORE PICTURESQUE SPEECH®

Spellbound

I have a spelling checker,
It came with my PC;
It plainly marks four my revue
Mistakes I cannot sea.
I've run this poem threw it,
I'm sure your please too no,
Its letter perfect in it's weigh,
My checker tolled me sew.

—Quoted by Pennye Harper

Marching Along

That sloppy little month sandwiched between the last frozen slice of winter and the first soggy slice of spring
—Elizabeth Westra

Icicles weeping silently in the last of the winter sun
—Rachel Sprague

Trees whispering an answer to the question of the wind
—Gina Flynn

Caucus of crocuses voting to end the winter
—Bonnie May Malody in *The Christian Science Monitor*

Fictionary

Nagagator: map-reading back-seat driver
—Ron Thorburn

Graffaxi: unsolicited comments received on a facsimile machine
—Lisa Hoyman, quoted by Mary Ann Madden in *New York*

Kleptocracy: corrupt government
—Douglas W. Payne in *Freedom Review*

Prima doughnut: cruller worth singing about
—Sonja Gleeson

Sellebrity: athlete in TV commercial
—Bruce Kafaroff

And Then There Was . . .

. . . the ram who charged over the cliff because he didn't see the ewe turn
—Bob Herguth in Chicago *Sun-Times*

. . . the disappointed fisherman who went back to the tackle shop demanding a rebait
—Bonnie May Malody

. . . the gold digger who married the prince with palace aforethought
—Kitte Turmell

Theme Songs

Army cook: "It Had to Be Stew"
Wrestler: "You Made Me Shove You"
Pastry chef: "There's a Whole Lotta Bakin' Goin' On"
—Susan Burritt

Picturesque Speechless

—Anthony Taber in *Audubon*

Do you have an item for "Toward More Picturesque Speech"? See page 4.

At Last!
Kibbles 'n Bits™ LEAN.

30% less fat* and the great taste dogs lean toward.

Introducing Kibbles 'n Bits™ Lean. It's 30% leaner in fat than the leading dry dog food. And it has all the great taste of Kibbles 'n Bits. In fact, dogs prefer the taste of Kibbles 'n Bits over the leading dry dog food 2 to 1. See if your dog isn't inclined to agree. New Kibbles 'n Bits Lean—the taste dogs are leaning toward.

*Than the leading dry dog food.

After circling and being unsuccessful in lowering his wheels, Fryatt requested permission to land. "Negative, circle." The planes continued landing. The bow of *Card* started to pitch a little more. Fryatt: "Permission to ditch." *Card:* "Negative, circle." Circling, Fryatt again requested permission to land. "Negative, circle." Fryatt: "I don't give a damn what you do, but do it fast!" All the returning planes were recovered and put out of the way.

It was almost dark, but we could see the sharp silhouette of *Card,* which by now was pitching more than the pilots would like but could handle with two wheels. Fryatt was given permission to land on deck with one wheel. Hundreds of eyes were on him as he came around and started his approach. Cries of "Go," "Come on," "Easy, easy," and "Do it" were heard around the ship.

All noise turned to one loud cheer when he was seen settling on the deck. But the Avenger continued to move along the deck. Within seconds the cheers turned to groans as we saw an airplane bounce over the bow and into the water. *Card* appeared to steam right over the unfortunate plane and crew. There were many sad sailors that night.

Things were brighter the next day. News from the *Card* was that Fryatt and his crew were uninjured. When Fryatt touched down, his tail hook missed the arresting wire. The belly of the plane bounced over the crash barrier which is supposed to stop a plane from going over the edge after a poor landing. The plane just kept sliding, hitting the bridge and ripping a wing off. Not stopped yet, the Avenger skidded along, stopping when it hit another Avenger, knocking it into the water. That was the plane we saw bounce off the deck. The pilot of that plane, Roger Kuhn, was Fryatt's roommate. He was pushing his plane in place to stop Fryatt's plane if need be, before it went off the deck. The buddy was knocked off with his aircraft and was picked up by the plane guard *Barry,* with only scrapes and bruises. Except for the loss of two Avengers, which could be replaced, the combined wishes and prayers of all those men did the job.

There was a little excitement early in the morning of October 15. *Card*'s radar had a solid contact at about two miles, dead ahead on our course. Any solid contact, followed by the gongs of general quarters, got the adrenalin pumping and everyone on their toes. Either *Goff* or *Barry* looked for it. It wasn't the *Borie,* but *Borie* would get its chance to search alone in only a couple of weeks. Anyway, whatever ship searched couldn't locate the contact with sonar and returned to its station.

By October 16, it was apparent we were now on our way to Casablanca. I don't know how we knew this, but we did. Something in the atmosphere seemed to change and also seemed to say, "Relax for a while." Captain Isbell forwarded another "well done" from Admiral King. I know it was not a game, but Isbell mentioned that our score was now twelve U-boats.

The gunner's mates found out on October 17 that gun no. 1 could not be moved. It was a good thing we were finished with that mission; in our business it could be disastrous to lose one-third of a broadside attack. Besides, who knew what was going to happen on our trip home.

On October 18 we tied up at the dock in Casablanca. It was determined that we would have to lift gun no. 1 to find and repair the cause of the problem. I think we must have radioed ahead since there were people waiting on the dock to help us when we tied up. Among other equipment there was a tall, mobile crane, without which we could never have gotten the gun in working order.

What happened next was another example of why the American service man did so well during World War II. If he wasn't trained for the job on hand, he improvised and somehow managed to get the job done. It took three divisions: gunner's mates, boatswain's mates, and fire control men. First thing, forget liberty, forget regular meals, and forget sleep. The following men are those that I remember working as a group with a cooperation that wouldn't be believed by a union chief: Gunnery—Dick Wenz, CGM; George Murphy, GM2c; Carmen Driver, GM2c; Oliver Pederson, GM2c; Kenneth Reynolds, GM1c; Eddie Johnson, GM2c. Boatswains—Walter Kurz, CBM; Oakley Hamilton, BM2c; Bill Schmalberger, BM1c. Fire Control—Bob Maher, FC1c; Jim Allegri, FC3c.

Allegri and I had to disconnect and later reconnect all the wires for remote control of the gun. The gunner's mates prepared the gun for lifting by removing all the necessary bolts. The boatswain's mates assisted whenever needed, especially if deck seamanship was required. We didn't only do our own jobs; everyone pitched in whenever he could, regardless of whether his division had responsibility.

We worked straight through for thirty-six hours or more, grabbing only a sandwich and cup of coffee when we could. At night we had other problems because the lighting was almost nil, forcing us to use drop lights and hand-held flashlights. We even used the old kerosene lanterns.

At first we worked full steam ahead. After about fifteen hours, we started to get weary, but then we seemed to get our second wind, and we were able to work at our peak again. At about thirty hours we all seemed to get a high on. We kept working, but we staggered about as if intoxicated, and we giggled about the silliest things. We found that a grease fit-ting hole didn't go completely through the base, and that caused the gun base to seize against the gun mount.

The gun was in place and in working condition only a few short hours before we were scheduled to get under way. Our executive officer, Lt. Phil Brown, gave us permission to sleep in as long as we needed and to ignore the cry, "All hands man your special detail." Phil was a good guy.

PART FOUR

⚓

Stand By for a Ram!

October – November 1943

TG 21.14 sailed out of Casablanca harbor at 1000 on October 20 while the working party just dreamed away. The first day was a lost day for me, but next day the regular routine of working and standing watch started. From our compass headings, it looked like we were on our way to the Azores again.

We lost about six planes on our trip east. I wondered what effect that would have on the antisubmarine activities. We were escorting a convoy again, but we had not seen it yet. That wasn't surprising because, judging from our results, the system of beating the U-boats to the punch had been working well. We heard that the other hunter-killer groups were doing nearly as well.

On October 25 there was a little stirring of the adrenalin. We received a message from the convoy that they had contacted a sub. One of their escorts chased it away. Just in case, our aircraft searched the area with negative results. Our experience, after escorting many convoys through sub-infested waters, had been that sub sightings by a merchant vessel were mostly whales, dolphins, and imagination, unless, of course, there had been a good solid hint like an explosion. We joined the convoy that day so the destroyers could refuel from an oil tanker. There were about fifty ships in the convoy. I was glad we were no longer doing that boring, but necessary, work. The convoy was "speeding" along at eight knots, unless you subtract time loss because of zigzagging. I missed watching the "slide for your ice cream" spectacular during fueling. Oil tankers did not make ice cream.

On October 29 we headed for a reported sub concentration. Previously such Huff-Duff reports were accurate, so our level of alertness stepped up a bit. We refueled (all escorts) from *Card,* another sign of getting ready, with the usual ice cream exchange. Aircraft activities seemed to be increasing, but that could have been just imagination and jitters. I knew one thing: it was wet and cold. It even snowed for a while. We also found out why it was so cold. We were only seven hundred miles from Greenland.

October 30 we woke up to heavy rains and rough seas that seemed to get rougher with time. Everyone seemed to be in a mood of expectation.

Something had to happen soon. I can't understand how they did it, but even with the weather as it was, the submarine search patrols went out. VC-9 was one great bunch. If they were assigned to ships like the *Lexington* and *Saratoga,* they would still have half a flight deck remaining after landing. Lieutenant (jg) Fryatt spotted a U-boat and immediately attacked. U-boat headquarters had recently issued an order for U-boats to dive at once if they were attacked by aircraft. Their previous orders had been to stay on the surface and fight, but the success of hunter-killer groups had proved too costly. The wise skipper of that boat heeded his advice and dived. Fryatt's bomb missed.

"Two bogies on the surface." After the report, he descended to five hundred feet and stayed behind the boats, *U-91* (type VIIC U-boat) and *U-584* (type VIIC U-boat) until more of the *Card's* squadron could arrive. We then heard a sudden, "They're shooting at me!" And indeed they were; both boats were cruising about a mile apart and firing at him, but their attack was ineffective.

U-91 wisely submerged and escaped just before two more Avenger aircraft arrived, piloted by Lieutenants (jg) Balliett and MacAuslan. As the planes closed in, Fowler and Balliett each dropped a Fido, one on each side of *U-584.* The attack proved to be deadly as *U-584* went to the bottom a few minutes later.

Because of the pilots' reports, Captain Isbell thought the escaping sub was a milch cow. With that in mind, the *Borie* was ordered to search for her.

Captain Hutchins informed us over the sound system that we had "volunteered" to search for the escaping U-boat. Amidst the cheers of all hands, at sunset and with moderate seas, we set off toward the area of last contact. We young bucks, dumb and happy, were really excited. We were the hunters, not the hunted, and it was an exhilarating feeling for all of us. Most of us stayed at our battle stations even though we weren't at general quarters.

When we arrived at the designated area, we went to general quarters and started searching with both radar and sound gear. In my battle station, just above the bridge, I could hear the steady pinging of the sound gear. PING . . . PING . . . PING . . . PING . . . as the outgoing sound pulses were lost in the vastness of the distant water. At 2010 I suddenly heard the cry, "Radar contact, bearing 095 degrees, range sixty-five hundred yards!" Earl Potter had detected something on the surface. Of course we couldn't

One of two U-boats (probably *U-584*) caught on the surface by the pilot of an Avenger. (Official U.S. Navy photograph)

see anything that far away in the dark, but we all looked anyway. With a hard turn to a heading of 095, the *Borie* crashed through the waves towards the enemy at a speed of twenty-two and one-half knots.

At almost the same time, the enemy detected us. We were in a perfect position for them to fire a stern shot, but we lucked out. With the obvious success of hunter-killer groups, the sub had recently been converted to an antiaircraft U-boat. The after torpedoes had been removed to provide more room to store antiaircraft ammunition. (Commanding officer of *U-256* Wilhelm Brauel told me years later that we would have been dead except for that.)

We maintained radar contact, and at seventeen hundred yards we opened up with star shells. The sky came alive with bright flares. In the meantime, the sonar kept up its monotonous pinging. Nothing was seen. I heard, "Radar contact lost." Almost at once we heard, ping-boing, ping-boing, the sound of returning echoes, followed instantly by the report, "sound contact," by our sound operator, Bob Manning. The sub had submerged and we lost radar contact, but at exactly the same bearing we obtained sound contact.

Slowing down to fifteen knots, we made a depth charge run after losing underwater contact at 150 yards. Bombs were dropped, and along with them a light marker float. Suddenly, one hell of an explosion rattled our ship and blew our fuses.

Few of the crew were aware of what happened next. The underwater explosion caused our sound gear to fail, and we lost our contact with the sub. Manning and Radio Technician Duke headed for the lower sound room; they located the faulty fuses, replaced them, and headed back to their battle stations. The sound gear was up and operating once again.

Below us a steady hand entered notations in the log book of our undersea enemy:

23:30	Surfaced, Course 240-D.
23:30	Destroyer 270-D, bow left, location 80-D, approx. 3,000 meters.
23:32	Destroyer shoots flares over boat, boat recognized.
23:33	Submerged.
23:36	At 110 meter take 6 to 8 depth charges on starboard side, silent speed, stopped all auxiliary engines, no more propeller noise heard.

Within minutes we were heading for the light marker, and again I heard the return sound echo, along with Manning's cry, "sound contact," followed by the range and bearing. We detected the odor of oil as we approached for and made the second attack.

One report indicated that the sub was on the surface, but no one on the flying bridge saw it. We made sound contact again, however, and the captain ordered another depth charge attack. Again we lost sound contact.

Another entry in the U-boat's log book described damage inflicted by our attack:

01-Nov.	
00:00	Depth 170 meters Destroyer propeller noises audible from port side, 10 close depth charges, taking water at

> bow-room, boat falls through to 220 meter. Only by
> blowing diving tank #3 able to hold boat. Run away
> at North/West, ASDIC detection, torpedo tube #2
> floods and empties into boat through leaking
> torpedo tube door.

We searched for three hours for evidence of destruction but found nothing. Captain Hutchins radioed back to the *Card,* "Scratch one pig boat." We all thought we had destroyed the milch cow. The *U-91,* however, was long gone. In fact, she was not a milch cow at all. We had been battling an attack submarine, the *U-256* (type VIIC U-boat), and she, too, was not sunk. After the war we found out that *U-256,* under the command of Oberleutnant Wilhelm Brauel, had managed to make it home to Germany in spite of suffering severe damage. *U-256* was unable to maintain a constant depth, but in spite of that it escaped by flooding and sinking to six hundred feet, then blowing out water and rising to two hundred feet (so we couldn't see them). The U-boat continued that until it was out of our detection range. Our blown fuse was also lucky for *U-256.*

That episode was one of those strange twists of fate; because the *U-91* escaped, we found and damaged the *U-256.* And because *U-91* escaped, fate was soon to deal us an even bigger hand.

Knowing that we were in an active U-boat area, we continued hunting. Bingo! "Radar contact, bearing 170, range eight thousand yards," called Manning, who was also operating the radar gear. Captain Hutchins immediately ordered, "All ahead full, come left to course 170." Our helmsman responded, "Left to 170, sir."

The sea was moderate, it was about 0200, and the ship's speed increased to twenty-seven knots. The whole crew felt the excitement building. At about two thousand yards we lost radar contact, but again we heard the returning echoes.

We got the order to release depth charges. Because of a malfunction, all the depth charges in the two racks rolled into the ocean at once. The resulting explosions lifted our stern and caused the ship to surge forward. We believed the job was done. Nothing could survive that, right? Wrong.

Looking back toward our marker flare, I was the first to see it: the conning tower of the *U-405* (type VIIC U-boat). I cried out, not in true navy fashion, "There it is—about forty feet to the right of the flare!"

We made radar contact and turned on our twenty-four-inch searchlight. Using radar bearings, we were able to keep *U-405* (not one of the

Wilhelm Brauel, commanding officer of *U-256*. Well-loved by his crew, who still call him father.

U-256 converted to an antiaircraft submarine, a conversion that may have saved the
Borie from destruction because the stern torpedoes had been removed.

two escaping subs) illuminated for the entire one-hour battle that was
to follow.

The conning tower appeared just off the port quarter, and we could see
the image of a large white polar bear. Only gun no. 4 could bear on the
target. As I remember, we got the order to fire as we moved away to
regain sound contact. When we turned and moved in at twenty-five knots,
the range was then one thousand yards.

As leading fire-control man, my battle station was director pointer,
and Jim Allegri was director trainer. In director-controlled fire, the director aimed and fired the main battery in unison, with pointer (me)
pressing the firing key. As all the guns came to bear, the order was given:
"Commence firing!" I pressed the key, and three four-inch projectiles
exploded as one in the vicinity of *U-405*'s main deck gun, obliterating it
before its crew could man it. Depending on the range, the main battery
gunfire control switched from director control to local control throughout the battle. As the main battery continued, the twenty-millimeter guns
opened up with devastating power, made even more spectacular by the
one-in-five tracer bullets that made it possible to follow all the streams
from the machine guns.

Watching the results of the converging streams of twenty-millimeter
bullets was both horrifying and fascinating. While the four-inch projectiles

The crew of *U-256* on October 31, 1943. CO Wilhelm Brauel is at center, wearing a white hat. Note the sawfish logo of the Ninth Submarine Flotilla (*U-664* was also part of the Ninth Submarine Flotilla). In May 1992, I was a guest of most of these men in Germany.

yielded terrific explosions, I really believe the machine gun fire sweeping across the deck was what finally doomed *U-405*.

Apparently *U-405* could not submerge as it tried to escape into the darkness, with men manning their machine guns. In the first few moments, our machine guns wiped them off the platform. For some reason, men came out of a forward hatch, about five at a time, and made an impossible dash of about thirty feet to get to their guns. None of them made it, as they were knocked bodily over the side, arms and legs flying. They kept trying, however.

The speed and evasive tactics of *U-405* were very impressive as we tried to maintain a parallel course to keep all guns bearing on target. The sub's turning circle was smaller than ours, and I learned later that she could do seventeen and one-half knots on the surface. *U-405* made good use of both those features.

When I was not busy I watched the sub as it tried to point its torpedo tubes in our direction, or perhaps just to escape, twisting and turning first in one direction and then the other. Captain Hutchins managed to keep the guns bearing most of the time in spite of our larger turning circle.

At one time, I was sure we were going to collide, not ram. I don't know if we attempted to ram that time, but I could see we were on a collision course, almost parallel. I realized then the high surface speed of the *U-405*. Just as we were about to collide, the U-boat appeared to turn on all its power, picking up enough speed to pass us. Looking down, I could see clearly the faces of the Germans still on the bridge.

We kept up a continuous fire, with all guns that could bear, giving the *U-405* a monstrous hammering. Many of her men were dead, and damage was extensive, especially to the conning tower. I wondered how long they could endure the savage beating.

At one time, a number of Very pistol rounds appeared to come from the conning tower, which was a recognition signal unknown to any of us. It seemed also that *U-405* either stopped or at least slowed, almost dead in the water. A man appeared on the bridge in the bright shining beam of our searchlight and started to wave his arms in crossing movement. Fate again interceded. Shortly before, a gun captain's telephone lines had become entangled in the empty shell cases that were by then rolling all about the deck. Frustrated, he had torn the phones off and thrown them to the deck.

Seeing the man on the deck of *U-405* waving, Captain Hutchins commanded, "Cease fire." But the galley deckhouse four-inch gun continued to fire. Hutchins then tried to shout directly across to the gun crew, and we on the flying bridge could hear plainly, "Cease fire, cease fire." Unfortunately, no gunner could hear above the noise on the galley deckhouse, and the big gun continued to boom out its deadly fire.

Watching that one man standing alone amidst all the destruction, with big guns firing, was awesome. It was not to last. Within a few moments his body stood there momentarily, arms extended over his head, then his head just disappeared. It was a sight that was to give me nightmares for months. Had the tangled phone lines caused the man's death? Had he been the bravest of the brave volunteering to expose himself to give a signal of surrender? We will never know, for the *U-405* picked up speed again and started evasive maneuvers.

The battle continued much as before, with *U-405* attempting to get away, or train a torpedo tube at us, or both. Meanwhile, we were trying to close range either to ram or to fire K-gun depth bombs.

"Stand by for a ram!" Our gunnery officer, Lt. Walter Dietz, gave the order to me to relay to the rest of the gunnery division over the fire-control phone system. The last five minutes or so had been frustrating but exciting. Because the range had closed to almost point blank, we were unable to use the gun director. For a short time we were only spectators.

I watched at first as if it were a game, the beautiful arcing tracers of the twenty-millimeter guns and the smashing four-inch projectiles hitting the sub or careening off the rounded hull into the darkness as a dull red, wobbly glow. I saw the German sailors knocked over the side as they tried to man their machine guns. As one went over, another would take his place.

Stand by for a ram! The command brought me back to reality. I passed the word to the men at their battle stations. Then I stopped the instant chatter on the system from all stations as I anticipated more urgent orders.

Looking over the wind screen, only about three feet high, I could see our bow crashing up and down, rapidly closing on *U-405,* still in our searchlight beam. I thought that if we hit the sub at that speed I would sail right over the screen and on down to the forecastle. I got behind the range finder and placed my hands on it in front of me. Then I thought, "Hell no, this way I'll get my face smashed." I moved in front and put my arms over the range finder behind my back and prepared for the crash.

As we got closer and closer, with as many of our guns firing as we could bear on the target, I watched and waited for the inevitable sudden stop.

From my vantage point I could see everything. I could see the no. 1 gun crew (bow gun) and wondered what they were thinking, as they would be the closest to the sub when we collided, bow on, and the most likely to be fired on just before ramming. I could see the Germans in the bright light still trying to muster some kind of defense, scurrying about in and near the conning tower.

Closer and closer we came, and I watched the sub get larger and larger. I held my breath, waiting for the crash. Almost at the moment of impact, the *U-405* made a sudden turn to the port side, trying to run parallel to our course and make us miss. The move was too late. We went at the U-boat at about a thirty-degree angle. I closed my eyes, held my breath, and prayed. Sneaking a peek with one eye, I saw our bow about to crash into the U-boat and the fear in the eyes of one German as he tried to get out of the way. Holding tighter, I waited—nothing. I looked up and saw that we were astride the sub with our bow just forward of her conning tower. Just before impact a large wave had caused us to rise above and over the U-boat's deck.

For a moment there was a stunned lull in everyone's action and thoughts. Then all hell broke loose on both sides. To our regret, the flying

An artistic rendition of the *Borie* astride *U-405*. My battle station is just below the searchlight.

bridge had no small arms, so except for phone messages, we were only spectators. In fact, from our vantage point directly below the large search-light and looking straight down on the conning tower encircled by the bright beam, it looked more like a Hollywood epic than an actual battle.

I could see the polar bear symbol clearly on the forward part of the conning tower and also the machine guns the Germans had been trying to keep manned. One quadruple mount and four single mounts were firing sporadically.

Ed Johnson started in with his twenty-millimeter mount, depressing it so that he had to shoot away the wind screen before he could fire into the men on deck. Although the action report says otherwise, my recollection is that no four-inch gun could be depressed far enough to bear, so all firing came from the twenty-millimeter guns and small arms. Upon hearing the ram order, Dick Wenz had broken open the steel small arms locker and passed the weapons out to men on deck. The story in some newspapers that he broke open the locker with his bare hands was a bit exaggerated. He did, however, break it open with a fire ax.

I saw Johnson open up and watched the first shots explode through the wind screen. I saw Walter Kurz throw a four-inch shell case into the group of men standing in the conning tower. From below on the bridge, I saw a flash from a Very pistol and watched a bright ball of fire arc across into a man's chest. He went down and rolled over with his chest still burning.

Lieutenant Dietz repeated an order from the bridge to me: "We will not board, we will not board." I then got a call from the fire-control man at the fire-control switchboard, which was isolated by dogged down hatches. "What the hell is going on up there?" He didn't know we had rammed the U-boat.

I saw one German reach out with his hand as if he wanted help to board the *Borie*. No one offered to help. Small wonder, as they were still firing their machine guns!

Two gallant crews were engaged in fierce battle using every kind of weapon at their disposal. There were no signs of fear or disorder anywhere in the *Borie*. Everyone went about his duty with the utmost confidence, and I felt great pride in being a member of the crew. I was to be even more proud by the time the action was over.

I was stunned and impressed by the size of the *U-405*. From my vantage point I could see that it was almost as large as our ship, or about three hundred feet long, which was large for a sub during World War II. I had also been impressed by its speed and maneuverability before we mated with it. As we slid apart, how I don't know, I was again impressed by those features of *U-405* in the ensuing action, especially in light of the damage it had suffered. The *Borie* was to do well also, in spite of serious damage. After the war I found out that *U-405* was only 220 feet long. It's strange what stress will do to judgment. The whole crew was sure at the time that it was at least three hundred feet long, and it got bigger and bigger as the years went by.

We, on the flying bridge, did not know it yet, but the *Borie* had sustained serious underwater damage to both engine rooms. In fact, the forward engine room was already flooded by the time the boats separated.

U-405 made a mad dash into the night, with us firing whatever guns we could bring to bear. We saw a four-inch shell explode in the sub's starboard diesel exhaust, but it didn't seem to slow the boat as it took advantage of its smaller turning circle to open the range to about five hundred yards. We fired one torpedo but missed because of one of those fast, tight turns.

The *U-405* continued circling in a turn that our ship could not match. The *Borie*'s movements were also hampered by the flooded engine room. We did, however, manage to maintain our murderous shelling, killing twenty to thirty of the sub's crew as they tried to man their deck guns.

Unable to close our range because of the U-boat's circling maneuvers, Captain Hutchins used a clever ruse. He ordered the searchlight turned off. Of course, the sub immediately tried to escape into the dark. We tracked it by radar until it reached a position to our advantage. With our entire starboard gun battery bearing on the fleeing boat, Captain Hutchins ordered, "On searchlight, commence firing!" The *U-405* once again came under heavy, damaging gun fire.

We started to close to ram again, but before we hit, the *U-405* turned into our starboard quarter. Seeing an advantage, Hutchins swung our ship hard to port, using both rudder and engines. This move brought us to a parallel course with *U-405* and within range of our depth charge projectors. Three charges were fired, one over and two short—a perfect straddle. All three exploded at thirty feet. We not only heard the explosions, but since we were dead in the water they almost knocked us over. What we felt was nothing compared to what it must have been like in the U-boat. *U-405* appeared to lift out of the water and almost stopped, thus ending what appeared to be an attempt to ram us. But to our surprise the Germans came on again, heading directly into our still heavy gun fire. They just would not give up.

Again they turned toward our stern and apparently tried to get away. But their speed just wasn't good enough. They were on our starboard side, heading away aft of us. To close on them again, we started to circle around to our port side so at first the range opened up. At about seven hundred yards the remaining torpedoes in the port tubes were readied. Hutchins ordered, "Stand by to fire torpedoes." Tom Neary, sitting on the torpedo tubes, matched pointers with the torpedo director, a unit that measures the proper angles so that the fish hits the target. At just about firing time, a full salvo of the main battery let go, with the usual jolt throughout the ship, causing an engine room hatch to jump open. The open hatch stopped the tracking of the tube just before we heard the whoosh of the fish leaving its tube. All of us on the bridge could see the shallow torpedo charge through the water on its deadly mission and we watched in fascination as yet another tableau emerged. That time fate was on the side of *U-405*. The torpedo slithered by her bow, missing by about ten feet.

In the meantime, we were still firing all guns. Shortly after the torpedo miss, we again hit the sub's starboard diesel exhaust, which finally brought it to a standstill. Out of the conning tower came a shower of Very stars, splashing the night with white, red, and green lights indicating that

the Germans were at last ready to surrender. That time we all heeded
Captain Hutchins's order to cease fire, and the night was silent after more
than an hour of mayhem.

One or two men appeared and started to throw yellow, two-man,
rubber life rafts into the water. They were tied together and gave the appearance of a string of very large hot dogs. The *U-405* was now settling
fast by the stern. What was left of the crew, about twenty, managed to get
off and over to their rafts just before the sub went down. An underwater
explosion rumbled soon after.

The German survivors in their rafts continued to fire Very stars as we
moved slowly towards them, still illuminating them with our searchlight.
We thought they were signaling another sub as a white star was shone in
the distance.

With the survivors just off our port bow, so close we could see their
faces, our sound man, Earl Potter, reported suddenly, "Torpedoes, bearing 220." Hutchins ordered, "Hard to port, heading 220, all available
speed." Unfortunately, that heading caused us to cut through the group of
survivors. I vividly remember seeing the face of one young boy straight
below me. His eyes were wide and his mouth open in a silent scream as
he extended both arms, hoping we would pick him up. It was not to be,
however, as someone reported seeing the torpedo traveling down along
our port side. *Borie* withdrew to rendezvous with TG 21.14 at best speed,
seventeen knots on the starboard engine. Underwater damage to the hull
made the port engine useless.

All of us were troubled because of leaving the survivors and hoped
the other sub would come to their rescue. Once that October 1943 battle
was over, they no longer would be the enemy but brave fellow seamen. In
light of what was to follow, they would not have been much better off and
probably would have caused the *Borie* to lose men.

We had been without sleep for twenty-one hours, but our ordeal
wasn't over yet. We left the battle area, making ten knots at best, and
turned in evasive zigzags to get away from a possible sub attack while
we assessed damage, which was considerable.

Only then did we on deck learn about the courage and ingenuity of
the men who had been struggling below decks during the battle. When
we rammed the *U-405,* a large hole in the forward engine room started
to flood immediately. While the guns boomed above, the men below,
in water up to their necks, had to maintain ship's speed as others tried to
repair the damage. The battle went on as the water level climbed.

The *U-405* in earlier times. Note the polar bear logo on the conning tower. Crewmen are leaning on an eighty-eight-millimeter deck gun, a formidable weapon.

Of these German officers, Chief Warrant Officer Joacha (second from left), Chief Warrant Officer Scheikhardt (second from right), and Chief Warrant Officer Schlobohm (at right) went down with the *U-405*.

The forward engine room was manned by Chief Engineer Lt. M. R. Brown, Chief Machinist Mate Bill Green, Machinist Mate 1c (throttle) Dan Dailey, Machinist Mate 2c (phone to bridge) Bill Howard, Machinist Mate 2c (on bridge phone) Ben Hugo, and Fireman 1c (oiler) Mario Pagnotta.

Borie had been moving at high speed when she hit *U-405*. At the jolt and sudden stop, the bridge to engine room annunciator exploded. All speed changes were given by phone. Howard, receiving orders from the bridge, passed them to Lieutenant Brown and to Dailey for compliance. Earlier, when the order, "Stand by for a ram" was received, both Howard and Dailey thought they were safe since they were about two hundred feet astern. They were surprised by the U-boat's diving fin slicing through the port side hull only about six feet away. Water rushed in immediately and began to fill the bilges. The forward engine room bilge pump was started but had little effect. Pagnotta worked the injection valves and applied the main circulating pump to the bilges, which greatly increased the

After a safe return from an earlier war patrol, the *U-405* crew celebrated with an allotted one bottle of beer apiece.

More of the *U-405* crew celebrate their earlier success and safe return with a nice meal on deck.

suction, but not enough. Sea water poured in faster than it could be pumped out. In a further effort to slow the rising water, a cross connection was made to the after engine room, and that bilge pump was added to the forward engine room pumps.

The damage control party, headed by Ed (Eggs) Robertson, carpenter's mate 1c, rushed to the forward engine room. The party consisted of Machinist Mate 2c Edd Shockley, Machinist Mate 1c Irving Saum, Machinist Mate 1c Ed Trenz, Carpenter's Mate 3c "Mingo" Concha, and Carpenter's Mate 3c Paul Brabant.

Attempting to close the holes caused by *U-405*'s fin, Shockley, Trenz, and Saum stuffed it with mattresses. Robertson shored the mattress plug with a four-by-six-inch beam. The feat was accomplished in an extremely tight space. Water level was maintained for a short time, but soon a "full astern" order was received (back off *U-405*). Then "stop," then "flank ahead both engines." *Borie* was clear of *U-405* and heading out of there. The added pressure of the high speed changes forced the mattresses out of the holes. Mattresses were not a viable solution. With all available pumps

Korvettenkapitän Rolf-Heinrich Hopmann, commanding officer of *U-405*, another well-liked CO. He went down with his ship.

The entire crew of *U-405,* shown during inspection. Except for a few transfers, all these men went down with their ship.

working, water continued to rise until it reached sea level. With engine room no. 1 out of action, Lieutenant Brown ordered all hands out. They had been running the ship in waist deep water with floating oil drums knocking about.

Damage was also experienced in the after engine rooms, but on a smaller scale. Steaming at seventeen knots towards *Card* and the escorts, the men in the after engine room also did an outstanding job in operating their plant. Water rose rapidly because the cross connecting valve to the forward engine room was still open. The valve was under the surface of the flooded engine room and under a submerged water tank. Irving Saum dove under the water, under the water tank, amidst rolling oil drums, to close the valve. He succeeded in a very dangerous effort, but broke his arm completing the job. Although water reached nearly to the floor plates, the leakage was brought within the capacity of the main circulator for the next few hours. *Borie* was able to move closer to the task force.

Although we were headed to join the group, we were not out of danger. I guess we were never out of danger after we contacted *U-256.* Our situation could be catastrophic. The water level in engine room no. 1

was equal to the level of the outside sea. The bulkheads between it and fire room no. 2 (forward) and engine room no. 2 (aft) were holding against the immense pressure. The boilers were hot, making steam for starboard engine no. 2 to get us the hell out of there. Fear arose that if the bulkhead between the engine room and the fire room gave way there could be an explosion when the cold water hit the hot boilers. Even if there was no explosion, having two compartments filled with sea water wasn't a pleasant thought.

Robertson, Concha, and Brabant started shoring operations to prevent that. Concha and Brabant gathered wood shoring beams from the ship's supply while Robertson went below into fire room no. 2. Ed, climbing around the hot boilers, searched for solid backstops to place the ends of the shoring beams. He went deep into the ship, almost down to the keel, and decided to place the beams against the base of the boilers. He called out measurements to Concha and Brabant who sawed the beams to size and passed them to Ed. Robertson placed them between bulkhead and boiler base as the ship was knocked about. Everything ready, all three hammered the beams solidly in place. Lieutenant Dietz inspected the completed job and reported to Captain Hutchins, "Have no fear of that bulkhead giving way." The after bulkhead of engine room no. 1 also was shored, but it was an easier job—if any job below decks of a mortally wounded ship is easy.

The courage, intelligence, and ingenuity of those men was so widespread that day that it would be difficult to name all those involved. But the executive officer's statement in the post-battle action report said it all. "They, the crew, manned their stations and obtained the maximum efficiency from the equipment at hand. The complete disregard for personal safety, and the initiative shown by all hands was an inspiring sight."

No sleep was in store for our tired crew as we tried to make our way back to the *Card* group at a speed of ten knots. We radioed that information to the *Card*, still not knowing the severity of the damage. With the forward engine room completely flooded, we had lost all but emergency radio power, which was used to send our messages to the *Card*. That, too, did not last long. The loss of all electrical power would make it extremely difficult to run the ship and make repairs. We could not recover feed water for the boilers, so we began to fear that we "might be in a little trouble."

At dawn we found ourselves in a lot of trouble. Emergency radio power was gone, a heavy fog hemmed us in, and we were taking on water

Domingo "Mingo" Concha, carpenter's mate 3d class, enjoying a smoke break. A member of the damage control party, he was lost at sea. At right is Gerald Flynn.

rapidly. We had to use all available gasoline to keep the pumps running to try to stay ahead of the incoming water; none was available for our radio generator.

To stay afloat, Hutchins gave the order to lighten ship. All hands turned to. Bucket brigades worked at a furious pace. Specific pieces of equipment were ordered jettisoned. We dumped our boats. Saving ten rounds per gun, the gunner's mates threw over all the rest of the four-inch shells. They also threw several machine guns overboard. The torpedo men dumped their torpedo mounts—quite a feat. CBM Kurz cut away the bases of the torpedo tubes with an acetylene torch. The boatswain department let go all our anchor chain, which went to the bottom with a long, rattling roar.

Captain Hutchins called me to the bridge and gave me the order, "I want you to dump the gun director over the side, and I don't want it to come down on my bridge." I really had no idea what the gun director weighed, but considering its size and the fact that the base was made of bronze, a fair estimate would be between one thousand and two thousand pounds. The navigational bridge, below, extended about five feet out on both sides of the flying bridge. I could see no way to swing it out from above. In spite of serious doubts I replied, "Aye, aye, sir."

I cannot remember who helped us, but Jimmy Allegri and I could not handle the task alone. However, I do remember that the navy's jack of all trades, the boatswain's mates, were everywhere. Our bo'suns, Walter Kurz, CBM; Bill Schmalberger, BM1c; Oakley Hamilton, BM2c; and Harold Isenberg, COX, did a wonderful job clearing the decks. I'm sure that some of them helped Jim and me.

I disconnected all the wires coming from the base into the junction box on the bridge overhead. We then lifted the director with pry bars, inserting wedges wherever possible. Gradually the director started to lean to starboard until, finally, it was almost balanced on edge. For once the large waves were an advantage. As we rolled to starboard we all pushed; the director dropped neatly into the sea—without coming close to Hutchins's bridge.

By midmorning, still in fog and our headway dropping slowly but steadily because we were now using sea water in our boilers, it became apparent that abandoning ship was a distinct possibility. Hutchins ordered Chief Torpedoman Cronin to drop depth charges off the stern racks. I remembered once meeting a sailor who had abandoned a destroyer going down, only to be injured seriously when the depth charges exploded.

Two charges were dropped. They exploded at a shallow depth, lifting our stern and shoving us forward. Our already stricken ship rattled and groaned. Hutchins roared, "Set them on safe." We felt the concussion and surged forward again. Hutchins screamed, "God damn it, I said set them on safe!" Chief Cronin yelled back, "God damn it, they are on safe!" As I remember it, they had to remove the detonators to keep them from exploding.

At least once we thought we had heard the sound of an aircraft above the fog. It well could have been, because at 0650 the *Card* had launched four aircraft on antisubmarine patrol with orders to be on the lookout for the *Borie*. They could not see the *Borie,* or anything else. So at 0950 the aircraft still in the air were directed specifically to look for *DD215.* Because of the bad weather all airplanes were back on board the carrier by 1030 with negative results.

By that time the ship was practically stopped, and for the most part we were standing around, wondering when and if we would be found or whether another sub might get us first. After all, we were still in an area reported to have a heavy U-boat concentration. Waiting, listening, and hoping for the best, the whole crew now had time to realize what a hell of a predicament we were in.

Sometime before 1100, Lt. Bob Lord thought of collecting all the lighter fluid, kerosene, and alcohol aboard ship and using the whole mess to run the emergency radio generator. It worked!

At 1110 the *Card* received our message, sent out by Cameron Gresh: "Commenced sinking." The high-frequency radio direction finder did it again, and two Avenger aircraft set out to search the area along the bearing. Despite the limited visibility, Lieutenant (jg) MacAuslan spotted us at 1130; we were fourteen miles from *Card.*

Upon getting the report of our sighting, the *Card* group changed course to our bearing and sped towards us at a speed of eighteen knots. By the time they arrived, we were wallowing in the troughs of huge waves. We were happy to see our fellow warrior, the *Goff,* coming close at about noon. At last we were no longer alone in sub-infested waters.

We saw the *Card* catapult four aircraft that headed off into the four quadrants of the compass, presumably to sweep the area surrounding our task force, which was in a precarious position. We were dead in the water, the *Goff* was nearly so, and the *Card* was moving slowly with only one escort, *Barry.* The *Goff* came alongside, bow to bow, and attempted to pass over suction hose and handy billies. Someone finally decided that

Lt. Bob Lord, who thought of collecting lighter fluid and alcohol to use in the emergency radio generator. Lieutenant Lord was lost at sea.

Concerned crew members of the *Card* watch the foundering *Borie,* as fellow destroyers on the horizon steam toward her. The angle of the men walking on the flight deck gives some idea of the rolling sea.

these would be no help since we had no fresh water for our boilers, and the seas were too heavy for us to transfer water from other ships. We abandoned the possibility of towing because we had no towing engine, and we already had dumped our anchor chains.

At 1630, with the weather getting worse and darkness setting in, Hutchins had no choice but to abandon ship, even though we appeared not to be in danger of immediate sinking. With the bulkheads bulging and the waves getting larger, the danger of capsizing was always there.

Then began a most harrowing experience. At about 1630 Hutchins gave the order to abandon ship, with the seas running twenty feet or greater. I was on the flying bridge, just above the navigational bridge, and I heard the order before it was passed on to the crew. My first reaction was anger, as I was wearing a brand new red Kearny High School warmup coat my brother had given to me. Everyone on the ship, including the captain, had admired it.

Knowing that I had no choice, I dropped the coat on the deck and went to my abandon-ship station. We had thrown away our boats trying to save the ship. The life rafts on the starboard side would not move because of the high winds and towering waves. That was to become a serious problem later, when all hands were finally off the ship. I picked up an old kapok life jacket from the deck and slipped it on over a rubber one I had already inflated. A few minutes later, Ed Malaney came up to me and told me that his life jacket had broken. I gave him the kapok, acknowledging that I did not need two. As events later unfolded, I was wrong again. Regardless of my plight, however, Ed had a life jacket, and we both survived.

When I reached the port rail I found that men had already put out lines. Here goes anything! I crawled over the side, holding on to a line while the ship rolled to starboard about thirty degrees. Crawling down the side of the ship, I had to climb over a beading of armor about six inches thick. I had just cleared the armor when the ship rolled back to port; the beading hit me on top of the head and drove me deep into the water.

I came to the surface, spotted two life rafts about ten yards ahead, swam to the closest one, and hung on. The raft was overflowing, so I swam to the other one, which was almost empty. I had just reached it when I found myself crushed between the two rafts. When it felt like my chest was about to burst, I screamed, "Jesus Christ!" and the two rafts just drifted apart.

Dusk had set in, and although none of the rescue ships was in sight, we began to take the situation in stride. A petty officer holding onto the raft next to me told me that my life jacket was broken. As I was being crushed between the rafts, the pressure must have broken the holding clamps. The jacket was useless, and it soon drifted away.

There I was, life jacketless, and darkness meant that we would not be able to see a rescue ship, even if one came along, nor could it see us. What was worse, our raft was so full of men that we had to hold on to each other like a bunch of grapes while the raft rode up and down in the huge waves. No one seemed to realize the trouble we were in. We even joked about it and occasionally broke into song.

Suddenly someone saw the silhouette of a destroyer bearing down on us. We all started to cheer. But we soon stopped when we realized that no one in the ship had seen us. She was going to hit us with her bow, dead center. About thirty men were in (or holding onto) our raft, with about four sitting in the middle, one of whom was Tom Neary. Tom was one of those nice quiet guys who never appeared to be around but always got his work done. Fortunately for all of us, he was around that time. He

Ed Malaney, a great friend and shipmate. I gave Ed an extra life jacket I had picked off the deck. We both survived.

reached into his jacket and calmly pulled out one of those cheap flash-lights (that never worked) and flashed it towards the destroyer. It worked. The ship was *Barry;* it veered to port, but not soon enough. The starboard side of its bow hit our raft on the side opposite me. It was a terrible sight. Some men scrambled up the side of the ship—many were killed between the ship and the raft. I attempted nothing. Without a life jacket I knew I would get only one chance, and not a very good one at that.

After that pass, we remained alone in darkness again. The singing and horsing around had stopped; this was no longer a game. The *Barry* showed up again. That time the ship's crew saw us, or at least it appeared they were not going to hit us head on. To the best of my recollection, about a dozen men were still on, or holding on to, the raft, and we were all very wary.

In the cold angry seas, the *Barry* looked foreboding as its dark form approached us, crashing against the swells. The ship hit us again, but this time we were all on the far side of the raft, and no one was hurt. A mad scramble ensued as we all tried to climb aboard the ship. As far as I know, most made it by climbing on the raft and then jumping to the ship's rail. I was afraid to try at first. Another problem was that the officer who had been alongside me for a while was in bad shape. He had been fine before the *Barry* whacked us, but at the moment he was hysterical, and nothing I said or did helped. I hit him on the shoulder as the raft slid down the side of the ship to alert him, but he didn't respond. I now saw a screw guard approaching and I knew that this was my best chance and I had to go. I climbed up on the raft and crouched down, waiting. The *Barry* was in a roll away from us as the raft went under the guard. I stood up to grab it just as the ship started its roll back. It hit me on the back of the head. I was con-scious long enough to see the guard crush the officer's head against the raft. Then I was out cold.

I came to under the water, feeling the beat of the screws under my feet, my arms folded over one of the bars of the screw guard. Whether it was instinct or my stiff heavy jacket that kept me stuck to the screw guard, I don't know. The worst thing was that no one was there to help me.

I hung on and shouted, but to no avail. I remember thinking, "Only married three months and I'm going to die." Suddenly I felt tugs at my neck and looked up to see two brave men trying to save me. One man was on deck holding on to the other, who had climbed out on the guard. He had me by the back of the neck, holding onto my jacket and pulling as hard as he could, all the while shouting, "Let go!" But I was afraid that if his hands slipped I was a goner. I shouted back, "Bullshit; if you let go I'm dead!" I was soon convinced that he was my only chance for survival, so I let go and they hauled me aboard.

An excerpt from Babson's diary reads:

> A message just came in from the *Barry* and the *Goff* saying that between them, they have picked up one hundred and twenty five men so far. It is 2230 now. I hope that they are all picked up pretty soon as it is cold out there now. According to the engine room, the temperature is 49 degrees. The water is also rough. . . . We just found out that there are thirty five more men in the water. I heard the doctor say that if they are not picked up soon that they would not last until morning as the water is too cold.

Twenty-seven were lost and eight were yet to be picked up during the rescue attempt. I was one of those eight. I am quite sure that I was next to last picked up, at about midnight. At 2230 it had already been six hours since we abandoned ship. You would not believe how many times over the years I have been told that no one could last that long. Selig Sirota was still sitting on the raft when I bailed out.

I had been in the water for about seven and one-half hours, and I was stiff as a board and totally helpless. I could not move a muscle, so my rescuers dragged me by the neck across the deck, bouncing me over pipes and everything else. They began to look for a place to leave me so they could get back to their rescue work. They placed me in the head. Other men out there needed their help. I was just thankful to be alive.

Lying flat on my back on the deck would have been all right except that I could not move, and I was pressed against the port side bulkhead, under the urinal trough. Water was on the deck, and every time the *Barry* rolled to port, I had to hold my breath to keep from drowning.

During a lull, two men finally carried me down to the crew's compartment and put me on a lower bunk below the mess table. Just above me, on the table, was a huge dishpan filled with old soapy water and garbage. The rescue attempt had started at about evening mess time, and all hands went topside looking for survivors. Lying there, still immobile, I thought about all that had happened when suddenly the ship rolled hard to port and I found myself covered with dishwater and potato peelings.

Some time later (they told me it was about midnight) the ship's doctor and a medic came to see me, cleaned me up, and moved me to another bunk. Best of all, they fed me a large shot of legal brandy. That was the first

The morning after we were rescued, the gallant *Borie* was still burning near the bridge.

time I had ever had a legal drink aboard a ship. No time could have been better. I went off to sleep and didn't wake up until after daylight.

I was in pretty good shape and was able to get around. Now came the gathering of survivors to swap information about our shipmates, trying to find out who had made it and who had not. There were many hugs and many tears, and all in all it was a very emotional time. Of my three best friends, I knew only that Mousey had made it because he was on the *Barry*

Wallowing heavily in the troughs and reportedly in the center of U-boat groups, the *Borie*'s condition was deemed beyond salvage so orders were given to sink the ship.

with me. We received partial lists from the *Goff* but Jim Allegri's name and Bill Schmalberger's name were not on them. Later on, Jim told me that he and Bill thought I was dead. Someone had seen me crushed between the rafts and said that I could not have survived.

Although the storm had passed during the night, the sea was still quite heavy. We were surprised to see that the *Borie* was still afloat, although it was down by the stern and wallowing heavily in the troughs. However, we could not have stayed aboard, as the major bulkhead between the engine room and the fire room was bulging and could have given way at any time. It would have been chaos, trying to abandon ship in the dark with such heavy seas and a shortage of lifesaving equipment.

According to the *Card*'s action reports, we were in the approximate center of five reported submarine groups. *Borie*'s condition was so bad and danger from the U-boats was so great that salvage was impossible.

The *Borie* takes a direct hit from the bombs of a *Card* TBF Avenger. She went down vertically by the stern, keeping her bow afloat as long as possible.

Orders were given to sink the *Borie*. Torpedoes and shell fire hurtled toward the ship, but the heavy seas made both methods inaccurate. Bombs from the *Card*'s aircraft finally sank her. Although badly mauled by the previous battle and the heavy seas, she still went down as a valiant lady. It took three bombs close aboard before she went down swiftly by the stern at 0955.

On our previous trip we had rescued forty-four German survivors of the sunken *U-664*. We transferred them to the *Card* by pulley line, placing them inside canvas bags and pulling the bags across the water between the two ships.

We now found ourselves in a similar predicament. There were 22 *Borie* men on the *Barry* and 107 *Borie* men on the *Goff*. Destroyers were designed to hold only just enough men. Thus, we were to transfer to the *Card* by pulley line, an idea I did not fancy one bit. The transfer was to take place during regular refueling.

With the bag hanging on a block and tackle rigged between the *Barry* and the *Card*, we prepared to give it a go. We on the *Barry* at least traveled first class—one man at a time. Some men on the *Goff* went two at a time.

Survivors of the *Borie* being moved from the *Barry* to the *Card* by mail sack. I am in the upper center, holding my hat.

I climbed into the bag without a life jacket, and they closed the bag over my head with the draw string. I took off like a shot as the large group of men on the *Card* ran down the deck. My "friends," who almost died laughing, later told me what happened next. At the midpoint I came to a sudden stop. There I was, hanging in a mail sack about fifty feet above the

A *Borie* survivor goes from the *Goff* to the *Card* via air mail.

ocean, midway between two ships about fifty yards apart. When the ships rolled together I dropped like a rock. When they rolled away from each other, I went up like a rocket.

Just as suddenly I moved forward swiftly, only to be stopped again; that time my hands, knees, and face slammed against the *Card*'s deck. My patience had begun to wear thin by then, so when the bag came open I emerged from it screaming, "Jesus Christ, if it isn't one damn thing, it's another!" In reply the *Card*'s chaplain greeted me with, "Glad to have you aboard, son."

The *Card* crew treated us royally. They gave us the whole forward part of the ship as our quarters. Giving us their bunks, the *Card* guys slept in hammocks set up in the mess hall. Not having the foggiest idea how to string a hammock, it was a great arrangement for me.

We spent another week at sea, and it was fascinating to watch and be part of a carrier's operations. More important, it was a time the survivors could spend together, trying to find out all we could about the men who were lost. During that time, Ed Malaney took me to Captain Hutchins and reminded him he had promised to give five dollars to the first man who spotted a sub on the surface. I expected him to hit me on the head

Captain Arnold Isbell (right), CO of the *Card,* congratulates *Borie* CO Hutchins as he arrives aboard the *Card.*

since he had lost his ship, but he reached into his pocket and gave me a five dollar bill. All the survivors from my life raft signed it, and then Ed Robertson framed it for me while we were homeward bound. It now hangs on the wall of my office.

The stories about those who did not make it are compelling. One man who had not heeded the warning about not drinking the water in Casablanca contracted dysentery and was confined to his bunk. He was not seen abandoning the ship. A hospital corpsman, who had not turned in all his alcohol, had invited men (including me) for a drink or two of pineapple juice and alcohol. He was last seen drunk as a skunk, and no one saw him leave the ship either.

Those were the stories passed among the survivors. However, Captain Hutchins and the executive officer, Phil Brown, had made a thorough search before being the last to abandon ship. One other "true story" was that a "sailor's sailor," fearing he wasn't going to make it, gave his money belt to another sailor with instructions to give it to first sailor's wife. The friend died, but the first sailor made it. Also, Ensign St. John, former football coach at Kilgore High School in Texas, helped men aboard the heaving *Goff* while he held on to the screw guard until he was lost. Fol-

Survivors rescued by the *Barry* on the *Card*'s hanger deck. I am in the center of the front row, third from right. Mousey is on my right and Selig Sirota is on my left.

lowing the war, the Kilgore school system's stadium was named in his memory. The stadium is home to the Kilgore High School football team as well as Kilgore College. It is also the home field of the famous Kilgore College Rangerettes.

When we were near Norfolk and presumed out of danger, we held memorial services for our missing shipmates. Only then did the true impact of our loss sink in. We had lost twenty-seven shipmates, friends of three years.

The task force arrived in Norfolk, Virginia, on November 9, 1943, and received the Presidential Unit Citation. Captain Hutchins, who in true navy tradition had made one last inspection and seized the ship's colors before abandoning ship, won the Navy Cross. Two more Navy Crosses, two Silver Stars, and one Legion of Merit also were awarded. I got a new chapstick. I had lost mine when the ship went down.

Lieutenant Hutchins, last man to leave the ship, carried the *Borie*'s battle flag with him, here held by several survivors. Among them are Bill Green (second from left), CMM and recipient of the Silver Star; in the middle is Walter Kurz, CBM; and Lieutenant Hutchins (at right), recipient of the Navy Cross.

Survivors of the Borie *assemble on the flight deck of the* Card.

Heads bowed during a memorial service aboard the *Card,* survivors of the *Borie* honor their twenty-seven shipmates lost in battle. Lieutenant Hutchins is in the foreground; to his left is Captain Isbell. (Official U.S. Navy photograph)

Inspecting the Presidential Unit Citation pennant are (left to right) Lt. Comdr. Herbert D. Hill, USNR, CO of the *Barry;* Lt. Comdr. Howard M. Avery, USN, CO of VC-9 (composite air squadron); Lt. Charles H. Hutchins, USNR, CO of the *Borie;* and Lt. Comdr. Ira Smith, USNR, CO of the *Goff.* (Official U.S. Navy photograph)

Adm. Royal E. Ingersoll, USN, pins the Navy Cross on Lt. Charles Hutchins.
(Official U.S. Navy photograph)

Epilogue
The Navy and Afterward

⚓

After some administrative work was completed and we were issued new sea bags, we were off on thirty days survivor's leave.

Many of us arrived at Pennsylvania Station in Newark, New Jersey, at about 7:00 P.M. With a frenzy of hugging and kissing, we were greeted by a crowd of relatives and friends, no doubt raising the curiosity of all those nearby. Doris and I caught a cab, and we were soon at our home in Kearny.

Of course there were the expected emotional greetings from immediate family and close friends, but soon I was just enjoying my leave. All of the survivors were flabbergasted at the news coverage. Navy public relations must have contacted all the newspapers in the hometowns of every survivor because we all had the same experience. On the second day we were surprised to find our pictures on the front pages of local newspapers. We were recognized on the streets, in church, and in stores. It was heady stuff. A day or two before our leave ended, *Life* magazine appeared on the newsstands with the complete story of our battle. That is, as complete as security allowed.

We reported back at Norfolk on December 10, 1943, and were assigned a barracks to ourselves. With no duties to perform, the next two weeks were spent on liberty or hanging around the barracks. On Christmas Eve we learned our new assignments. We were disappointed; we had hoped to stay together and join a newly constructed ship. Although we did stay together, we didn't get the new construction—in particular, the USS *Borie (DD704)*. Our next ship was the USS *J. Fred Talbott (DD156)*. We traveled by Pullman car and boarded the *J. Fred* on Christmas Day. Newly promoted Lieutenant Commander Hutchins came aboard as our commanding officer.

It was to be seven months before USS *Borie (DD704)* was launched, July 4, 1944, and another two months before it was commissioned,

North Jerseymen Aboard Destroyer Borie Sunk in the Atlantic

DOMINGO CONCHA
Missing in action

James Allegri   Kenneth Reynold   Walter Reynolds   Arthur W. De Santos   William E. Howard Jr.

Mark Millionth Ammunition Box

Rutledge Co. of Montclair and Orange Celebrates Occasion at Plant Luncheons

George Rutledge Co. of Montclair and Orange, which made signs before the war, yesterday celebrated completion of ammunition box No. 1,000,000 for the Army. Free "ammunition box" luncheons were served the 300 employees at regular noon and supper hours. Workers wore special buttons signifying the event.

Congratulations were extended by Kenneth Nash of Caldwell, general manager of wartime production, and by his father, George Nash of Montclair, company president, as well as by production and

Robert Maher   Joseph Samphilip   Oakley Hamilton   Edgar Robertson

Irvington Reduces Child Care Fee

Cost to Parents of School Age Children Cut from 50 to 30 Cents

The daily fee for children sending two of three Irvington child care centers will be reduced from 30 cents to 20 cents beginning Monday, School Superintendent Libby told the Board of Education Wednesday.

Libby's announcement came when Louis Miraglia of the board asked for an extensive accounting of one of the centers. The accounting revealed the per-child cost of the program for four months ending October was $290.

Libby said application would be made today to the FWA

Local newspapers carried our pictures and the story of the *Borie*'s final battle, surprising us with the attention we received.

September 21, 1944. The new destroyer joined the Pacific Fleet on January 4, 1945, more than a year after *Borie (DD215)* went to her grave.

Borie (DD704) served with distinction, taking part in the Iwo Jima bombardment in January 1945. Joining Task Force fifty-eight, she participated in the Tokyo and Okinawa raids and in the raids supporting the occupation of Okinawa. Serving with Task Force thirty-eight, she took part in raids on the Japanese home islands from July 9 to August 9. On August 9, a Japanese suicide plane crashed into *Borie*'s superstructure, between the mast and the fire-control gun director, causing extensive damage, killing forty-eight men, and wounding sixty-six.

Borie DD215 survivors, especially fire controlmen and bridge hands, might well consider the often quoted thought, "Everything happens for the best."

My service was short and uneventful. *J. Fred Talbott* left Charleston in January for Casco Bay, Maine, sailing independently. We moored in Norfolk on January 6, 1944, for a week, and then resumed our cruise to Casco Bay, arriving on January 14. Days of drills and antisubmarine practice followed, but we left Casco Bay with anticipation. *Talbott,* in company with the USS *Babbitt,* joined the battleship USS *Nevada* to escort her to New

In addition to the newspapers and *Life* magazine, the account of the *Borie* gained further glory in comic books. This version was published in July 1944.

York. Liberty in New York! Not quite. As we passed New York Harbor, *Nevada* waved good-bye, made a sharp right, and proceeded on her own. *Babbitt* and *J. Fred Talbott* arrived in the great liberty port of Norfolk on February 9.

My last cruise on *J. Fred Talbott* started on February 13 as we joined the escort group of Convoy UGS-33, headed for Casablanca. Dull, dull, dull. We even fired guns no. 1, 2, and 4, just for the hell of it.

March 2, early morning—landfall. It couldn't be Casablanca, I couldn't smell it. Getting closer, it was obvious we were approaching the Straits of Gibraltar. Then I saw a large rock jutting out of the ocean. It looked just like the Prudential Insurance Company logo. I couldn't believe it. I thought, wait until I tell my brother, a Prudential employee, that there's a large Prudential rock sticking out of the Atlantic Ocean.

Machine gun batteries were manned before we escorted UGS-33 through the straits into the Mediterranean. There was some apprehension while all hands watched for the dangerous German E-boats. Released from escort duty well into the Mediterranean, the trip inbound had proved uneventful, but it had been exciting for a while thinking that something might happen. Reversing our course, we headed for the Atlantic in column. Leaving the column, we formed a line abreast, and all ships conducted a sound sweep passing through the Straits of Gibraltar.

Escorts *Bibb, J. Fred Talbott, Babbitt,* and *Badger* moored alongside Buoy fourteen at noon, March 3, in Casablanca harbor. Maybe the Germans were running out of submarines.

Early afternoon on March 7, *Bibb, J. Fred Talbott, Babbitt,* and one other ship sailed out of Casablanca harbor, forming a column after leaving the entrance. At 0012 the task force changed course to form a line abreast with an easterly heading, moving towards Morocco, south of Casablanca. General quarters were sounded at 0020. Operation Spangle commenced at 0030. Rumors aboard ship were that a submarine was supposed to place saboteurs or spies on shore in the area. True or not, Operation Spangle was fun.

At 0030 each of the five ships fired a star shell from gun no. 1, then dropped a depth charge. It was great to see the sky light up and hear the rumble of depth charges along the line of ships. With a small time interval between firing, we continued until we had fired eight star shells and dropped eleven charges. Making things more interesting, at one point a shore battery fired a couple of large shells at the ships. The projectile was large enough to be seen going overhead as a dull glow and heard as a wump, wump wump. To say that they missed would be kind as they missed by miles. Operation Spangle ended at 0230.

Forming a column, with *Talbott* fifth in line, we headed toward Casablanca, joining Convoy GUS-32 at 0800. The convoy sailed toward New York harbor. The days passed without incident. Relieved of escort duty at New York, all escorts proceeded in column to Boston Navy Yard, mooring at 1005 on March 24.

April 4, 1944, was a bittersweet day. I received orders for transfer to the Advanced Fire Control School at the Navy Yard, Washington, D.C. Further orders upon completion of my training were for transfer to new construction: destroyers. Exactly what I had wanted for a long time, but now I realized I was to leave my close shipmates of almost four years. Those friendships had been made even stronger when we shared the loss of our ship and shipmates. Fortunately the good-byes were short; I was given less than a half hour to leave the ship, which was about to get under way.

With orders to report at the school on April 24, Doris and I spent some time at home before leaving to search for a place to live during the eighteen-week course.

I did well in the fire-control course, which consisted of mathematics, electronics, fire-control optics, problem diagnosis, gyroscopic fundamentals, and all the fire-control equipment required for the main battery of a new destroyer. That comprehensive course was to provide the basics for my civilian career following the war.

Finishing the course with a final average of 90 percent, my orders were changed, and I reported to the Instructor's Training School (Fire-Control), Washington Navy Yard, the next day (same place, different building). The course covered basic teaching methods, lesson plans, and testing, but most of the time was spent giving practice lectures followed by a critique with the teacher. That course, plus the actual teaching experience that followed, also proved important to my civilian career.

I reported aboard the Navy Training School, Seattle, Washington, for duty as a fire-control instructor on Thanksgiving Day, 1944—four years to the day after our reserve unit left for who knew what adventures.

After I discovered that I loved teaching, the remainder of my World War II duty was a blast. When I made chief fire-controlman in early 1945, my military duties became much more satisfying. Never losing my love of teaching, about June 1945 I began to get itchy; I was afraid that the Japanese war would end, and I wanted to be a part of it. After more than a year, shore duty was no longer all that great, and after teaching the five-inch, thirty-eight caliber antiaircraft system for that entire period, I had complete confidence in my ability to take charge of such a system. Unknown to my wife, I requested transfer to Pacific sea duty. Almost at once I was assigned to what was touted as the largest carrier in the world. It was being prepared on the West Coast for the invasion of Japan. Best of all, her main battery was the five-inch, thirty-eight caliber system I had been teaching. The not-so-good news was that I was to report aboard in October 1945. I was excited as hell; I was getting the best of all duties (for me)—Pacific duty aboard a new carrier with a familiar gun system.

Fate, as it had so many times, once again changed my future. The United States dropped the atomic bomb. I'm ashamed to say it, but when the war ended, I felt cheated for an instant—but only for that instant.

The next day or so after the surrender agreements were reached, there was a large joyous parade, including the entire fire-control school. Wearing dress blues, white CPO hat, white gloves, white leggings, and white belt, and as commander of a marching group, I felt like General MacArthur. When I was given a sword to carry, I *was* General MacArthur.

Sailors have never been noted for marching. That parade was no exception. My company had a bagpipe band in front and a marching band to the rear. Not a good combination, even for good marching units. Nearing the reviewing stands, I cringed as I watched the white hats bobbing up and down, not more than several in unison. What a mess. With about fifty yards to go, the bagpipe band stopped playing; the marching band broke into "Stars and Stripes Forever." I damn near cried. The hats leveled off, rising and falling as one unit. I could not have been more proud as I ended my World War II naval service with the command "eyes right" and watched heads snap towards the officials.

Discharged and back in New Jersey by the end of September, I took some college courses under the G.I. bill and went to work for the Bell Telephone Laboratories as a laboratory assistant. From the first day I knew I had found my career. I worked with physicists, called members of the technical staff, doing pure research on almost anything that can be imagined. My first project, for example, was bombarding diamonds with electrons to study the properties of insulators. It was the nuts.

I continued taking evening college courses on job-related subjects, and I also enlisted in the Naval Reserve (my old outfit) again. I taught fire control again one night a week and went on one two-week cruise every year.

Here I am holding my son, Guy, who was born in 1952 in the naval hospital at the Naval Training Station, Bainbridge, Maryland, where I was on active duty.

The Korean War interrupted my career for two years, but my duty was fantastic. After completing a four-week refresher instructor's training course in Norfolk, I reported for duty at the Fire-Control School at the Naval Training Center, Bainbridge, Maryland. That center was primarily a recruit (boot) training center, and when they graduated, qualified personnel were assigned to the various schools. I reported for duty as a chief petty officer, and the only one who gets more respect in a boot camp than a CPO starts His name with G.

The tour of duty couldn't have been better. I was teaching again, living in naval housing (a three-room apartment), and driving a new automobile; life was enhanced by the birth of my son, Guy. Having only a minimum of military duties, I completed a course in naval electronics and also successfully finished the two-year college course offered (on base) by the U.S. Armed Forces Institute.

I had been apprehensive about how the time on active duty would affect my career at the Bell Laboratories, but I found it had enhanced my standing. Reporting back for work, I was promoted to associate member of the technical staff and assigned to work in the same laboratory and on

This flag of the Ninth U-boat Flotilla was presented to the *Borie* Association in 1990 by the former commanding officer of *U-256,* Wilhelm Brauel.

the same project. Now, however, I did the work independently. As before, I felt like a kid living in a toy store, and though I never told anyone, I would have worked for nothing, but I couldn't afford it.

One sad note was that Doris and I were divorced, by mutual agreement, in 1955. It was to be the best thing for all three of us—Doris, me, and Guy.

Without a day of wishing I was doing another type of work, I retired in 1983 as a member of the technical staff.

On behalf of the *Borie* Association, I give a speech to the former crew of *U-256* at their reunion in Rudesheim, Germany, in May 1992.

I married my present wife, Sandy, just prior to retirement. We left for Florida two days after I retired and settled in our new home in a beautiful retirement park.

In early 1984 I saw a notice from Bob Manning in a navy publication asking if anyone was interested in a reunion of the former crew of the USS *Borie (DD215)*. I got up from my chair and called him (after forty years). We worked hard for almost a year and managed to locate 123 men from the *Borie*. Sandy and I then went to work and organized a reunion that was held in the fall of 1985 in Orlando, Florida. It was a huge success, with more than sixty former crewmen attending and a total of about 120 people. Many tears were shed as old comrades greeted each other. The gathering of shipmates of long ago, especially if they have experienced battle together, is not the same as an old school reunion. One had to experience that to understand the camaraderie and deep feelings that develop among a ship's crew. No one can adequately describe it.

That this camaraderie still existed after forty-three years inspired me to form the USS *Borie (DD215)* Association in January 1986. We enthusiastically started with 123 former *Borie* crewmen who had boarded her from

On the fiftieth anniversary of the sinking of our ship, the USS *Borie (DD215)* Association held a reunion of former crew members of the USS *Borie (DD215)* in Washington, D.C. My wife Sandy and I placed a wreath at the feet of The Lone Sailor, at the U.S. Naval Memorial Center, honoring the *Borie*'s lost shipmates. The Presidential Color Guard presented honors.

1920 through 1943. The formation of our association provided me with an instant part-time job that still exists. We have had nine successful annual reunions, two of which were especially notable.

Our 1990 reunion in Delaware Water Gap, Pennsylvania, had as guests four World War II U-boat veterans. They were Wilhelm Brauel, commanding officer of *U-256;* Konrad Ellwart, executive officer of *U-256;* Otto Schutze of *U-3530;* and Konrad Mueller of *U-381.* You will remember that we dropped eighteen depth charges on *U-256,* so it was an interesting and unique experience to meet our former enemy face to face. Wilhelm presented the flag of the Ninth U-boat Flotilla to the *Borie* Association, and both Wilhelm and Konrad Ellwart presented official (1943) enameled pins with the swordfish logo of the Ninth Flotilla to all attending *Borie* men.

The *U-256* Association invited *Borie* crewmen to attend their reunion in May 1992. Sandy and I, Bill and Rita Howard, Ed and Thelma Lundin, and Chuck and Betty Gloady were welcomed in Rudesheim, Germany, by about thirty *U-256* veterans. We were treated more like visiting royalty than former enemies.

On the weekend of October 30–31, 1993, almost fifty years to the day since the *Borie* went down, we had our annual reunion in Washington, D.C. What better place to celebrate our continuing camaraderie and honor the memory of our departed shipmates than in the citadel of our nation's history. Sixty-three shipmates attended, with a total attendance of about 120.

The featured event of the reunion was honoring our departed ship-mates at the U.S. Navy Memorial Center with the presidential honor guard providing the honors. Sandy and I had the honor of placing the wreath at the feet of The Lone Sailor. That was followed by a member of the navy band playing taps.

This ends my tale of the *Borie* and its gallant crew. Those of us remaining will continue to gather for reunions, the Lord willing. Deeply cherished, our memories of bygone days will never be forgotten. We will forever be patriots, navy men, and *Borie* shipmates.

Appendix A

⚓

FINAL USS *BORIE (DD215)* ROSTER
MEN LOST AS RESULT OF BATTLE WITH U-405

Officers	Chief Petty Officers	Petty Officers	Enlisted
Lt. Robert Lord	William Shakerly, CQM	Frank Duke, RT1c	James Winn, S1c
Lt. Morrison R. Brown	Harold DeMaio, CWT	Frank Cituk, PH1c	Max Blane, S2c
Ens. Richard St. John	Ralph Long, CCSTD	Francis McKervey, Y2c	Opal Alford, S2c
		Domingo Concha, SF2c	Andrew Wallace, F1c
		William Mulligan, SC2c	William Medved, F1c
		Aguinaldo Pruneda, COX	Lawrence Francis, S2c
		Joseph Kiszka, WT2c	"D" "L" Tyree, S2c
		Warren Blouch, SC2c	Frank Swan, F2c
		James Fields, F1c	Daniel Pouzar, F2c
			Richard Tull, S2c
			Charles Bonfiglio, S2c
			Joseph Lombardi, F1c

SURVIVORS OF THE *BORIE'S* LAST MISSION
Chief Petty Officers

Truman T. Cook, CEM	W. J. Green, CMM	Kenneth M. Lucas, CMM	R. W. Wenz, CGM
F. J. Cronin, CTM	Walter W. Kurz, CBM	Elton C. Partin, CMM	

Petty Officers

James M. Aikenhead, SM3c

Ernest Gardner, STM2c

Richard B. Branch, WT1c

James K. Brewster, MM2c

Daniel A. Dailey, MM1c

Carmen L. Driver, GM2c

Edmund F. Fitzgerald, TM3c

Charles Flewelen, STM2c

Robert A. Maher, FC1c

Thomas J. Morris, EM3c

Kenneth L. O'Kelly, WT2c

Earl J. Potter, SoM2c

Walter R. Reynolds, TM2c

Christopher Shepard, CK1c

Anton Svetlecich, RM3c

Frank S. Zendzian, MM2c

James K. Gillet, RM3c

George P. Angelson, RM3c

James V. Holcomb, TM3c

Bill Howard, MM1c

Joseph Hummer, SC3c

W. N. Johnson, BM2c

Daniel Jones, STM2c

Warren R. Klotz, QM3c

Edward A. Lundin, TM3c

C. Lester Moultrop, SM2c

Richard W. Osean, MM1c

Wm. W. Powers, M2c

Edgar R. Robertson, CM1c

Irving R. Saum, MM2c

Edd M. Shockley, MM2c

Edward Trenz, MM1c

James Allegri, FC3c

Cameron C. Gresh, RM1c

George A. Brey, EM3c

James F. Clubb, RM1c

Arthur W. DeSaules, MM2c

Harvey C. Eldridge, MM2c

Thomas C. Fitzgerald, BM2c

Gerald E. Flynn, SM3c

Edward M. Malaney, SM2c

George T. Murphy, GM2c

Mario J. Pagnotta, MM2c

Michael Protz, EM3c

Joseph J. San Philip, SK1c

Martin R. Smith, RM3c

Oswald Williams, STM2c

Paul E. Brabant, CM3c

Oakley L. Hamilton, BM2c

John G. Hook, TM1c

Ben C. Hugo, MM1c

Harold J. Isenberg, COX

E. M. Johnson, GM2c

Lerten V. Kent, SoM3c

Woodard L. Landers, GM3c

Robert E. Manning, SoM2c

Tom F. Neary, TM3c

Oliver W. Pederson, GM2c

Kenneth J. Reynolds, GM1c

Wm. A. Schmalberger, BM1c

George J. Sturla, WT2c

Walter Yeager, MM2c

Deck Crew

Carl W. Banks, S1c

John R. Blaszczak, S2c

Robert D. Bradshaw, S1c

Charles H. Gloady, S1c

C. J. Beaulier, S2c

Joseph G. Blasco, S2c

Roy L. Chappel, S1c

John G. Gloady, S1c

C. L. Price, S1c

S. Sirota, S1c

Don M. Bird, S2c

Don H. Borte, S2c

Adolph F. Cook, S1c

Peter J. Gormley, SD2c

William R. Quarles, AS

Henry G. Blanck, S2c

Bernard J. Bozek, S2c

John J. Corcoran, S1c

Richard E. Lane, S2c

James Pate, S2c

Quincy R. Scott, S1c

J. P. Slatkevich, S1c

F. P. Welch, S1c

Glen T. Smoot, S1c

S. Sirois, S1c

Edward J. Staley, S1c

J. H. Schneweis, S1c

Vaino W. Skarp, S1c

Charles J. Stanton, S2c

Black Gang (Engine Room and Fireroom Crew)

Harley Adams, F1c

Kenneth M. Cook, F3c

Warren M. Gilpin, F3c

Wm. F. Megyesi, F2c

Joseph J. Poplawski, F2c

Joseph Ziemba, F2c

Carl T. Bomgardner, F3c

Robert E. Coulomb, F2c

James M. Glenny, F3c

John F. Mysona, F3c

Robert E. Slaight, F2c

Cyril J. Conners, F2c

Horace B. Farrar, F2c

C. W. Gore, F1c

Howard J. Peterson, F2c

David F. Southwick, F1c

Walter M. Converse, F3c

Robert J. Fuller, F1c

Daniel G. McKay, F2c

Frank J. Pollet, F3c

Andrew J. Taylor, F1c

Officers

Lt. Charles H. Hutchins (CO)

Lt. Phil B. Brown (EXEC)

Lt. (jg) Larry Quinn

Lt. Walter Dietz

Appendix B

⚓

Presidential Unit Citation

Presented to

Task Unit Twenty-one Point Fourteen

THE SECRETARY OF THE NAVY
Washington

The President of the United States takes pleasure in presenting the

PRESIDENTIAL UNIT CITATION

TO

TASK UNIT TWENTY - ONE POINT FOURTEEN

Consisting of the

U.S.S. CARD, U.S.S. BARRY, U.S.S. BORIE, U.S.S. GOFF
And
VC SQUADRONS ONE AND NINE

For services as set forth in the following:

CITATION:

"For outstanding performance during anti-submarine operations in mid-Atlantic from July 27, 1943. At a time when continual flow of supplies along the United States - North Africa convoy route was essential to the maintenance of our established military supremacy and to the accumulation of reserves, the CARD, her embarked aircraft and her escorts pressed home a vigorous offensive which was largely responsible for the complete withdrawal of hostile U-boats from this vital supply area. Later, when submarines returned with deadlier weapons and augmented anti-aircraft defenses, this heroic Task Unit, by striking damaging blows at the onset of renewed campaigns, wrested the initiative from the enemy before actual inception of projected large-scale attacks. Its distinctive fulfillment of difficult and hazardous missions contributed materially to victorious achievements by our land forces."

For the President,

Frank Knox

Secretary of the Navy

Bibliography

⚓

Books

Babson, H. H. *My Nine Cruises Aboard the U.S.S.* Card (*CVE-11*). Private publication, 1989.

Cremer, Peter. *U-Boat Commander*. Annapolis: Naval Institute Press, 1985.

Gannon, Michael. *Operation Drumbeat*. New York: Harper & Row, 1990.

Macintyre, Donald. *The Naval War Against Hitler*. New York: Charles Scribner's, 1971.

Morison, Samuel Eliot. *History of the United States Naval Operations in World War II.* Vol. 1, *The Battle of the Atlantic, September 1939–May 1943*. Boston: Little, Brown, 1948.

———. *History of the United States Naval Operations in World War II.* Vol. 2, *Operations in North African Waters, October 1942–June 1943*. Boston: Little, Brown, 1950.

———. *History of the United States Naval Operations in World War II.* Vol. 10, *The Atlantic Battle Won, May 1943–May 1945*. Boston: Little, Brown, 1956.

Roscoe, Theodore. *United States Destroyer Operations in World War II*. Annapolis: Naval Institute Press, 1953.

Werner, Herbert A. *Iron Coffins*. New York: Holt, Rinehart and Winston, 1969.

Y'Blood, William T. *Hunter-Killer*. Annapolis: Naval Institute Press, 1983.

Official Records

National Archives, Washington, D.C.:

USS *Borie* Log Book 1939–1943, Record Group 24, Records of Naval Bureau of Personnel Deck Logs of U.S. Warships.

U-256 Log Book Entries; translated copy provided to author Maher by Wilhelm Brauel, commanding officer, *U-256*.

Naval Historical Center, Washington, D.C., Operational Archives:

USS *Borie* Action and Damage Reports, November 8, 1943.

VC-9 Antisubmarine Report No. 31, October 30, 1943.

VC-9 Antisubmarine Report No. 32, October 31, 1943.

Interviews and Correspondence

Brauel, Wilhelm, commanding officer, *U-256*. Personal correspondence and numerous conversations.

Giese, Otto, junior officer, *U-405* prior to *U-405*'s battle with USS *Borie*. Personal correspondence and numerous conversations.

Kurz, W., USS *Borie*, petty officer and gun captain, galley deckhouse. Personal correspondence of February 28, 1987, and numerous conversations.

Manning, R. E., USS *Borie*, petty officer and lead soundman. Personal correspondence of November 11, 1986, and numerous conversations.

Personal conversations with Konrad Ellwart, executive officer, *U-256*; Otto Schutze, *U-3530*; Konrad Mueller, seaman, *U-381*. Also, conversations with about twenty former crewmen of *U-256* during *U-256* veterans reunion in Rudesheim, Germany, May 1992.

Index

⚓

SAILORS' JOURNEY INTO WAR

was composed in 12/13.3 Perpetua on a
Power Macintosh using QuarkXPress;
at The Book Page, Inc.;
printed by sheet-fed offset on 50-pound Lions Falls Turin Book Natural stock
(an acid-free, totally chlorine-free paper),
Smyth sewn and bound over binder's boards in ICG Kennett cloth,
and wrapped with dust jackets printed in two colors on 100-pound enamel stock
by Thomson-Shore, Inc.;
designed by Diana Dickson;

THE KENT STATE UNIVERSITY PRESS

Kent, Ohio 44242